MADE IN WALSALL
THE TOWN OF 100 TRADES

MADE IN WALSALL
THE TOWN OF 100 TRADES

MICHAEL GLASSON

TEMPUS

*To the craftsmen and craftswomen of Walsall, past and present.
May they continue to flourish!*

Frontispiece: A weary-looking worker at Eyland's buckle factory in Lower
Rushall Street *c*.1900. The large pots would be filled with buckles in the
annealing process, which involved heating the metal items and then cooling
them very slowly in order to relieve internal strains in the structure of the
metal. The Children's Employment Commission examined child workers as
young as ten at Eylands in 1843, and found them working a twelve-hour
day, tongue-filing, buckle-filing and 'nibbling buckle ends'. (Photograph
courtesy John Griffiths)

First published 2005

Tempus Publishing Limited
The Mill, Brimscombe Port,
Stroud, Gloucestershire, GL5 2QG
www.tempus-publishing.com

© Michael Glasson, 2005

British Library Cataloguing in Publication Data.
A catalogue record for this book is available from the British Library.

ISBN 0 7524 3566 3

Typesetting and origination by Tempus Publishing Limited.
Printed in Great Britain.

Contents

Acknowledgements

In preparing this book I have received a great deal of help and encouragement from a large number of people. A steady stream of old photographs, trade catalogues, company histories, personal recollections, private research notes and other material was readily made available to me, for which the book is much the richer. I am most grateful to all of the people listed below for their kind support and enthusiasm.

Stebbing Shaw wrote of Walsall in 1798 that 'being tinged with the smoke and manufacturing vicinity, this town has often been looked upon with ignominy and contempt, but surely without just reason... it surely deserves to be better known'. It remains true to the present day that the remarkable achievements of Walsall's craftsmen and women, and their energy, skill and inventiveness, have rarely received the recognition they deserve. I will be delighted if this book goes some small way towards redressing this imbalance.

My grateful thanks to: Mrs Pat Andrews, Frank Baines, Jen Beardsmore, Ian Bott, Dominic Bubb, Mike Butler, Geoff Crowe, Craig Eccleston, Graham Evans, Mrs Evans, Mrs Margaret Foster, T. Gameson & Sons, John Griffiths, Mr Grimley, Sheila Hennings at the Black Country Living Museum for her help with Chapter 5, Leon Jessel OBE, Malcolm Jennings at Stokes Forgings, Andy Middlebrook, David Mills at Walsall Leather Museum, The Old Hall Club (www.oldhallclub. co.uk), David Owen, Margaret Parker, Stephen Parkes, Penkridge Ceramics, Bob Perry, Chris Pickford, Allan Preston and the Crabtree Society, Richard Roberts, Malcolm Robinson at Ibstock Brick, Mr and Mrs Sanders, Sheila Shreeve MBE, David Wakefield at BIP, Walsall Local History Centre, *Walsall Observer*, Walsall Security Printers, Mrs Joan Waltho, Mrs J. Watkins, Brian Wheat, Nigel Wiggin for his help with Chapter 3, and Stuart Williams.

Introduction

The roots of Walsall's history as a great manufacturing centre can be traced to long before the Industrial Revolution. When John Leland, Antiquary to King Henry VIII, visited Walsall in 1540 he found a town busy with industrial activity. Coal, ironstone and limestone were all being dug, and 'many smiths and bitmakers' were hard at work making small metal wares. Some of this activity was already long established even when Leland wrote. Coal and ironstone mining, for example, are mentioned in the early fourteenth century. 'Adam the bloomer', mentioned in a document of about 1300, was probably an early smelter of iron, and John Sporier, created a burgess of the town in 1377, was almost certainly a spurrier or spur maker. John Brasier, who was created a burgess at the same date, was probably a maker of brass pots and pans and candlesticks. In short, Walsall people have been making things for a very long time, and industrial activity of one kind or another has been a constant presence for at least 700 years.

Walsall's early development as a centre for metalworking is not altogether surprising. Much of the western half of the Borough sits on the exposed section of the South Staffordshire coalfield. Coal could be quite literally picked out of the ground in places, and the famous Ten-Yard seam, one of the richest coal seams in Britain, lay close to the surface. Associated with the coal measures were extensive beds of ironstone. The ironstone at Rushall, two miles north of Walsall, was said to be of exceptional quality, and well suited to making the best metal wares. Charcoal, essential for smelting iron, was almost certainly being produced from local woodland, much of it long since cleared, but remembered in such names as Wood End, Reedswood and Walsall Wood. To the east of the town, stretching up onto Barr Beacon, lay a belt of common and scrub known from the thirteenth century as the Colefield, 'the open land where charcoal is produced'.

Early maps show the Walsall landscape as one of small and scattered communities, many of them evidently built on land cleared from heathland and scrubby waste. Though most of these communities have long since been absorbed into the Walsall conurbation, 'green', 'heath' and 'end' place-names such as Short Heath, Druid's Heath, and Darlaston Green still abound. Goscote, first mentioned in the thirteenth century and meaning 'the hut or cottage in the gorse', is especially evocative. Historians have noticed how many areas rich in heath and waste – for example, the Hallamshire district around Sheffield and the Potteries in North Staffordshire – gave rise to early industrial development. These were often areas of pastoral farming, with weakly developed manorial control, and plenty of opportunity for younger sons or incomers to build a cottage on a smallholding carved from the waste. Such encroachments were numerous in Walsall and as early as the sixteenth century the waste was becoming highly fragmented. Making a living from farming on Walsall's generally unrewarding soils, in an era before the advent of modern fertilisers and the tractor, must have presented a challenge. A second occupation such as digging coal and ironstone or practising a craft such as bit making could be a vital source of additional income to those living on the margins.

By 1700 an impressive variety of metal working trades was being practised in Walsall and its surrounding villages. Inventories show that there were specialist makers of nails, buckles, locks and edge tools, and workers in copper, brass, tin and pewter. Probably the largest group of craftsmen, however, were the loriners, or makers of saddler's ironmongery. Plot's account of the Walsall lorinery trade, published in 1686, reveals that many of the loriners were highly specialised. The making of a single spur, for example, required the skills of four craftsmen, each responsible for producing a different part. Similar levels of specialisation were to be found in the making of bits, stirrups, buckles and metal saddle parts. Such a degree of specialisation indicates that items were being sold over a wide area, and, as Marie Rowlands has argued in her important study, probably in very large quantities. The streets of Walsall must have rung with the sound of the loriners' hammers, and strings of packhorses laden with lorinery and other small metal wares would have been a familiar sight on the roads surrounding the town. The population of the Borough trebled in the century between 1650 and 1750, when the town clerk noted that the inhabitants 'are chiefly buckle makers and other working trades'.

After 1750 the pace of change gathered speed, especially in the output of essential raw materials. Local production of coal, ironstone and limestone was boosted by increased use of steam pumping engines, allowing the working of deeper pits and mines. The first steam pumping engine had been erected at Tipton in 1712, but after 1750 they became more numerous and more efficient. Within the local iron industry several significant developments helped to increase output dramatically. Some of these developments, such as the shift from smelting with charcoal to smelting with coke, and the use of steam engines to supply the furnace blast, were popularised by John 'Iron Mad' Wilkinson, whose furnace at Bradley, on the south-western boundary of the Borough, was one of the industrial sights of the age. Production of pig iron in South Staffordshire increased hugely so that by 1806 the region was producing a fifth of the country's total output, and by 1830 Staffordshire had overtaken Shropshire to become the chief iron-producing county in England. Blast furnaces were erected in many places in the west and north of the Borough – for example at Darlaston, Pelsall and Birchills – and numerous wrought ironworks sprang up making bar, rod and sheet iron. Many of these were sited close to canals, which provided a further stimulus to trade. A meeting was held in Walsall in 1770 to petition for the construction of a canal specifically 'to render the conveyance of coal, corn, ironstone, limestone and other produce less expensive'; by 1800 Walsall was well connected to the canal network, and a wharf had been opened at Town End.

Despite these developments a visitor to Walsall town centre even as late as 1850 would have found little evidence of the 'dark satanic mills' usually perceived as being synonymous with the Industrial Revolution. Walsall remained a town of small workshops rather than factories. The largest factory in the Borough was probably that of Moses Eyland & Sons, makers of buckles and spectacles, in Lower Rushall Street. Eyland's factory comprised a row of once-elegant Georgian two- and three-storey houses, which had been knocked through and extended. The domestic origins of this factory remained apparent throughout its history, and the site has recently been converted back to housing. More typical of Walsall were small backyard two-storey workshops, usually approached via a narrow tunnel entry, where perhaps half a dozen men worked at making lorinery or other small metal wares by hand. The same was true of Willenhall, where the lock industry predominated, of Darlaston and its gunlock trade, and of Bloxwich, which had become a centre of awl blade making. Despite the increased use of steam power in the extractive industries and the smelting of iron, the use of hand tools prevailed in most of Walsall's industries.

With the coming of the railways – the Grand Junction reached the outskirts of Walsall in 1837 and the South Staffordshire followed in 1847 – Walsall manufacturers had improved access to markets for their products, and the Borough's trade became increasingly international in character. In the 1860s the locksmiths of Willenhall had a flourishing trade with Australia, New Zealand, India and China. Walsall's loriners were supplying the gauchos of South America with spectacular silver-plated spurs and bits, and such specialities as lasso rings and bombillas (metal tubes for drinking maté, the gauchos favourite drink). Closely associated with the lorinery trade was the leather trade. In 1821 there had been just thirty-three leatherworkers in the town. By the 1860s the trade was employing over 1,000 men and women, and Walsall had overtaken Birmingham to become the country's leading provincial centre of saddlery and harness making. Much of the

Market (High St.), Walsall.

At the geographical heart of the Borough is Walsall High Street, seen here in about 1905. Weekly markets have been held here since 1220. Metalworkers were prominent among the early citizens, and many of them probably lived in the immediate vicinity of the High Street. This superb townscape was largely destroyed in the 1960s when Walsall's historic buildings were seen by 'some key' decision-makers as an impediment to economic progress.

production was for export, Australia and South Africa being especially important markets. In the last two decades of the nineteenth century Walsall became the great international emporium for horse goods of all kinds, and local manufacturers produced splendid catalogues of their products, such as Hampson and Scott's 'Equine Album', often considered to be the finest catalogue of horse equipment ever published. It runs to over 250 pages, and includes every possible item for the horse and stable, from nosebags to dung baskets and 'Hampson's Imperial condition powders'.

Despite its relatively rapid growth, leatherworking remained only one amongst Walsall's rich diversity of trades, and Victorian and Edwardian descriptions of the town usually stressed the wide range of products being made. Thus, in 1896, Walsall was described as producing:

… saddlers and coach ironmongery, buckles, chains, curbs, bits and stirrups with plated and other mountings, bridles, saddles, harness, collars and all the necessary trappings for horses and carriages, also locks, bolts, keys, pulleys, brushes, spectacles: there are also a number of brass and iron foundries, iron, galvanised iron and iron tube works, several corn mills and tanneries…

Darlaston, meanwhile, made:

… bolts and nuts, all kinds of screws, railway fastenings and general ironwork, roofs, bridges, and girders, all kind of wrought and cast ironwork, files, latches, axle pulleys, hat and coat hooks, oddwork, wire gauges and gunlocks, all of which are exported in large quantities. There are also malt kilns and brickfields, and several extensive ironstone and coal pits…

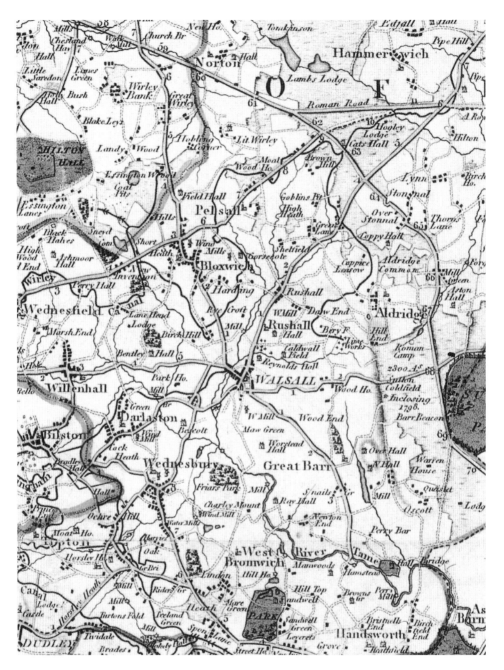

The Walsall area in 1798. Yates' map shows the distinctive settlement pattern of the region, with numerous small common-side hamlets, and the occasional nucleated village. Although much reduced by encroachment, the waste was still very extensive. It would have been possible to walk from Aldridge Common via Brownhills to the gates of Shugborough Park on the far side of Cannock Chase – a distance of almost 15 miles – without meeting a hedge. As the map notes, the Coldfield, the belt of wasteland to the east of Walsall, was about to be enclosed. Yates also shows the partially completed canal network, including the new Walsall canal opened in 1799. Additions continued to be made to the system until as late as 1847.

When Lloyd George visited in 1907 he commented that Walsall had: 'a greater variety of trades than probably any town in England'.

The early twentieth century saw the rise of new trades such as electrical engineering and plastic moulding, and a number of long-established trades adapting to changed circumstances. One of the biggest challenges to Walsall's trades in this period, and especially those connected with supplying the horse, was the coming of the motorcar. The adaptability of Walsall's craftsmen and women is a constant theme throughout Walsall's history, and this attribute was tested to the full in the years after 1900 as the 'horseless carriage' became increasingly popular. Saddlers and harness makers turned to making light leather goods such as bags and purses and gloves, and coach and carriage builders became motor-body builders. Saddlers' ironmongers – who had traditionally made bits and stirrups – began making other metalwork such as bathroom fittings and motorcar lamps. The automotive components industry rapidly established itself as a major local employer, with Rubery Owen completing their first motorcar chassis as early as 1896, at the very birth of the British motor industry. Metalworking in its many guises remained vital to the local economy. In 1931 two-fifths of the male working population were engaged in manufacturing. One in four male workers (almost 9,000 individuals) were employed in metalworking. The second largest manufacturing occupation was leatherworking, accounting for around 5 per cent of male workers. Manufacturing and coal mining together occupied almost half of Walsall's male working population (48 per cent). Amongst women in paid employment, the picture was slightly different, with leatherworking being the single biggest occupation, accounting for one in six. Textile working employed one in seven, or just over 2,000 women.

During the Second World War the skills of the local workforce played a vital if largely unsung part in the war effort. Leather flying helmets and jackets, camouflage nets for the Desert Rats, tanks for Spitfire fighter planes and parts for the Mulberry Harbours were just some of the items produced in Walsall. After the war Europe's devastated economy offered little competition to British manufacturers. The UK was still producing 20 per cent of the world's manufactured exports in 1954 and many Walsall firms were prospering, selling everything they could produce. However, by the 1960s the country was slipping behind its competitors in terms of productivity, and imports were beginning to eat into the home market. The 1970s were a painful time for many local businesses, with the international oil crisis leading to recession and soaring inflation. In some cases, such as Rubery Owen, these problems were compounded by strikes and disruption among the workforce. A period of crisis followed in the 1980s, as some of the Borough's largest and most celebrated companies, such as Old Hall, closed for good. Others survived, but in much reduced form, sourcing an ever-increasing percentage of their stock from overseas. Unemployment soared to over 50 per cent on some estates, and parts of the Borough became a wasteland of abandoned factories. Darlaston, with its concentration of large engineering companies, was especially badly hit, losing an estimated 20,000 jobs. Bruce George, the MP for Walsall South, described Darlaston in 1985 as 'an industrial graveyard, a pile of rubble and memories. It makes me weep for the people.'

The future of manufacturing in the West Midlands continues to be the subject of much debate. Low-wage economies in the Far East have unquestionably had a huge impact on many sectors of British manufacturing in recent years. Nevertheless, Walsall's long industrial history suggests that it has several strengths, which should stand it in good stead. The inventiveness of local people has frequently been demonstrated, and there are many world firsts that originated in the Borough, for example the first stainless steel tableware and the first pressed steel motor chassis, developments that have quite literally gone around the globe. The world's first self-adhesive stamp was designed and produced by Walsall Security Printers in 1964 and today the company produces millions of stamps for the Royal Mail and some sixty foreign countries. The ability to adapt is another strength in Walsall's industrial history, which will be increasingly important in future. It was well demonstrated by the manner in which many of the town's loriners expanded into saddle making in the early nineteenth century, and by the response of many of the saddlers in turn to the coming of the motorcar in the early twentieth century.

Walsall has also been receptive to people with new skills and energy. To take just a handful of the most conspicuous examples, the town's largest factory in the 1890s was that of John Shannon & Sons, founded by a Scots draper. In nearby Goodall Street a fellow Scot, John Leckie, operated the town's largest saddlery and harness factory. The Borough's two largest industrial employers of the twentieth century were both 'incomers': J.A. Crabtree, the electrical engineer, hailed from Rochdale in Lancashire and A.E. Owen, who co-founded Rubery Owen, one of the largest manufacturing concerns in the Midlands, was from Wrexham in North Wales. Finally, the superb craft skills that many local people possess are by no means redundant in the twenty-first century, as British manufacturers focus increasingly on small volume, highly specialised production. Walsall's leatherworkers and metalworkers have worked to demanding specifications for centuries and their exceptional skill has often been commented on. Plot remarked in 1686 how 'very nice' (in the sense of precise or fastidious) the town's loriners were, and in the leather trades it is outstanding craftsmanship, coupled with a readiness to adopt technical innovations (such as the use of computer-aided design and manufacture to produce saddle trees) that has helped Walsall retain its position as the world's leading centre for saddle making.

These four themes of ingenuity, adaptability, receptiveness and exceptional craftsmanship run through this book. They suggest that, challenging though manufacturing conditions are likely to be in the age of the global economy, local people will continue to excel at making things, as they have for the past seven centuries, and that Walsall's proud claim to be a town of 100 trades will remain true for many years to come.

Note: In defining the area covered by this book, I have followed the modern (post-1974) boundaries of the Metropolitan Borough of Walsall.

Further Reading

The Industrial History of Walsall

Allen, G.C., *The Industrial Development of Birmingham and The Black Country*, Frank Cass and Co., 1966.

Anon, *South Staffordshire (Illustrated), Biographical and Commercial Sketches*, Robinson and Co., n.d., (1899).

Clark, Howard D., *Walsall Past and Present*, Walsall Chamber of Commerce, 1905.

Crompton, John (ed.), *A Guide to the Industrial Archaeology of the West Midlands Iron District*, AIA, 1991.

Currie, CRJ *et al.*, *A History of Walsall*, Walsall MBC, 1988. An offprint of the *Victoria County History*, vol.17. Although it excludes many areas of the modern Borough, this is nevertheless the single most useful published source of information for Walsall's industrial history.

French, Ann, *Walsall Werk*, Walsall MBC, 1997.

Lewis, Marilyn and Woods, David, *The Book of Walsall*, Barracuda Books, 1987.

Palliser, DM, *The Staffordshire Landscape*, Hodder and Stoughton, 1976.

Pearce, Thomas, *The History and Directory of Walsall*, 1813, reprinted by Walsall MBC, 1989.

Timmins, Samuel (ed.), *Birmingham and The Midland Hardware District*, Robert Hardwicke, 1866. Includes sections on limestone and coal mining, iron working, the Willenhall lock trade and the Walsall leather trades.

Williams, Ned, *Black Country Folk at Werk*, Uralia Press, 1989.

Williams, Ned, *More Black Country Folk at Werk*, Uralia Press, 1990.

Greenslade, M.W. and Jenkins, J.G., *The Victoria History of the County of Stafford*, vol.2, OUP, 1967. Includes detailed accounts of the history of lock and key making, iron working, and limestone mining.

An atmospheric view of the Walsall Canal near Pleck Road in 1942. The canal acted as a magnet to large wrought ironworks, which lined both banks.

From Out of the Ground

Benson, John (ed.), *The Miners of Staffordshire 1840–1914*, Keele University, 1993.
Green, H.E., *The Limestone Mines of Walsall*, The Black Country Society, 1977.
Rollins, Brian, *Coal Mining in Walsall Wood, Brownhills and Aldridge*, Walsall MBC, 1994.

Iron and Steel

Anon, *The Story of The Old Works, John Harper and Co. 1790–1949*, privately printed, 1950.
Anon, *An Industrial Commonwealth*, Rubery Owen Ltd, 1951. (History of Rubery Owen).
Gale, W.K.V., *The Black Country Iron Industry*, The Iron and Steel Institute, 1966.
Gould, J., 'Excavation of a fifteenth century iron mill at Bourne Pool, Aldridge', in *Transactions of Lichfield and South Staffs. Arch. Soc.*, vol.XI, 1971.
Griffiths, Samuel, *Griffiths' Guide to the Iron Trade of Great Britain*, 1873. New edition, David and Charles, 1967.
McDonald, Leonard, *Rubery Owen Holdings Ltd. Archive*, University of Warwick, 1997.
Rowlands, M.B., *Masters and Men in the West Midland Metalware Trades*, Manchester University Press, 1975.

Old Hall

Bennett, Michael, *Old Hall Stainless Steel Tableware 1947–1984*, The Old Hall Club, 2004.
Coatts, Margot, *Robert Welch, Designer – Silversmith*, Cheltenham Art Gallery and Museums, 1995.
Welch, Robert, *Hand and Machine, Robert Welch, Designer, Silversmith*, privately printed, 198

Leather

Glasson, Michael, *Walsall Leather Quarter Trail*, Walsall MBC, 2001.
Glasson, Michael, *The Walsall Leather Industry*, Tempus, 2003.
Glasson, Michael, *200 Years of Walsall Leather* (second edition), Walsall MBC, 2003.
Mills, David, *In the Leather: Walsall Leatherworkers Remember*, two volumes, Walsall MBC, 1997 and 2002.
Waterer, J.W., *Leather Craftsmanship*, G. Bell & Sons, 1968.

Locks and Keys

Evans, Jim, *100 Years Plus of Keymaking – The History of Arthur Hough and Sons Ltd*, privately printed, 1998.
Glasson, Michael, *Willenhall Town Trail*, Walsall MBC, 1986.
Halstead, R., *The Story of Walsall Lock and Cart Gear, 1873–1923*, privately printed, n.d.
Stenner, Brian, *The Lockmakers. A Century of Trade Unionism in the Lock and Safe Trade*, Malthouse Press, 1989.

Miscellaneous

Anon, *Growth of a Group: A History of the BIP Group 1895–1949*, BIP Ltd, 1949.
Beetle Magazine, 1935. (The house magazine of BIP).
Champ, R.C., *Ahead of Time, The Story of Transport Built in Walsall,* Walsall MBC, 1993.
Dingley, Cyril S., *The Story of BIP 1894–1962*, BIP Ltd, 1963.
Lloyd, K.J., *The Highgate Brewery*, The Black Country Society, n.d. (*c.*1982).
Tilson, Barbara, 'The plastics industry in Birmingham and design in bakelite, beetle and melamine' in Barbara Tilson (ed.), *Made in Birmingham, Design and Industry*, Brewin Books, 1989.

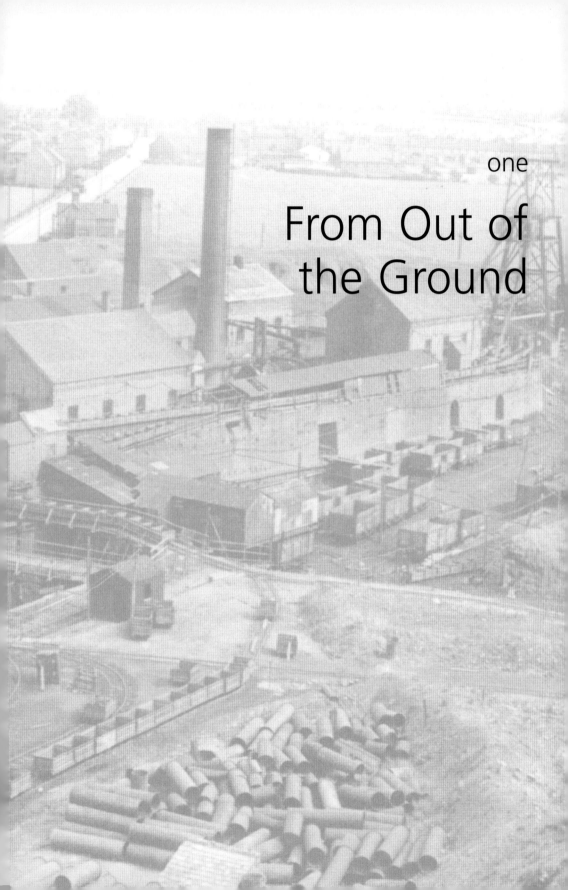

one

From Out of
the Ground

'At Walleshaul be pittes of se coles, pittes of lyme that serve also South Toun (Sutton Coldfield)
4 miles of. There is also yren owre.'
(John Leland, *Itinerary*, *c*.1540)

Walsall's wealth of easily accessible mineral resources has been the foundation of many of its most important industries. Coal, iron ore, limestone and clay have all been worked from early times.

Limestone outcrops can be found at many places across the Borough. The stone is easily worked, and it is possible that it may have been quarried in Roman times. However, the local limestone is generally friable and not especially well suited to use as building stone. The main use of the stone in the Middle Ages seems to have been as lime for mortar: for example, fourteen cartloads of Walsall lime were supplied for the repair of a mill in Warwick in 1417–18. At a later date lime was also being used as an agricultural fertiliser, to lower the acidity of soils, and Plot describes at some length the processes used to burn it in Rushall in the late seventeenth century. Walsall limestone was also being used as a flux in the smelting of iron, and with the growth of the Black Country iron industry this gradually became the main source of demand. From the late eighteenth century onwards the workings became much more extensive, helped by the newly built local network of canals, which provided much improved transport. Pumping engines enabled deeper mines to be worked, and they were certainly being used at Rushall by 1800. As demand from the booming local iron industry outstripped supply, extensive areas of Rushall and central Walsall were quarried or mined in the search for limestone, sometimes destroying existing buildings in the process.

Coal was also being worked in Walsall in the Middle Ages. The lords of the manor of Walsall agreed in around 1300 to share the profits of any mines 'as well as seacole, as of iron'. In the succeeding centuries it seems likely that literally hundreds of shallow pits were dug to work the exposed section of the South Staffordshire coalfield in the western half of the Borough. Preparatory work for the construction of the Black Country route in the 1980s revealed a honeycomb of previously unmapped workings between Bentley, Darlaston and Willenhall. As with the working of limestone, large-scale exploitation of the coal seams began in earnest in the late eighteenth century, helped by increased use of steam pumping engines, improved transport networks, and growing demand from the iron industry, which had largely abandoned charcoal in favour of coke for smelting by 1800. Demand was so great that by the second half of the nineteenth century much of the South Staffordshire coalfield had been exhausted, or was so badly flooded as to be unworkable, and mining companies were being forced to explore the much deeper seams of the Cannock Chase coalfield, in the northern half of the Borough and beyond. Pelsall, Aldridge, Brownhills and Walsall Wood all saw the development of deep pits after 1850. At Walsall Wood the colliery, which began production in the 1870s, became the biggest employer in its immediate area, and the population of the village doubled between 1871 and 1891.

Iron ore was often worked alongside coal. The coal measures in the Walsall area conveniently included beds of both clay and ironstone, such as the 'White Ironstone' and 'Gubbins Ironstone'. References to local bloomeries – primitive furnaces in which the iron was smelted to produce a spongy 'bloom' of iron – suggest that ironstone was probably being dug from the fourteenth century. From 1561 Walsall ironstone was being used by Lord Paget in his pioneering blast furnace at Cannock, and by Sir Francis Willoughby in his furnace at Middleton near Sutton. Many of the pits seem to have been close to the town centre. In the following century there was extensive working of ironstone at Rushall. Plot, writing in 1686, praised the quality of the ore here, 'of which they make all sorts of the best wares', and he noted that it was being worked across much of the parish including in the park and at Moss Close, near to the present-day site of the Arboretum. With the increased use of pumping engines in the late eighteenth and nineteenth centuries, it was possible to work deeper seams of coal and iron. Large integrated companies such as the Darlaston Steel and Iron Co. emerged, which combined the mining of ironstone and coal with the operation of their own blast furnaces and rolling mills. Production of ironstone in South Staffordshire soared and in the late 1850s reached a total of almost one million tons per annum, before falling away as reserves became exhausted.

The legacy of centuries of extractive industry has been a mixed one. By the late nineteenth century most of the more easily worked deposits had been worked out, or were unworkable due to flooding, leaving a wrecked landscape over much of the western half of the Borough, especially between Willenhall and Darlaston, where it seems as if every inch of ground must have been turned upside down in the search for coal, clay and ironstone. In Walsall the closure of the last town-centre limestone mine around 1903 left a mass of collapsing underground workings, which, until as recently as the 1980s, blighted a broad swathe of land to the north and west of the town centre. It has taken many years and a great deal of money to remove the worst of these eyesores, to level spoil heaps, cap shafts and stabilise old workings. But in environmental terms there have also been gains. Many of the Borough's most attractive landscapes, such as the Arboretum, Hay Head Wood and Pelsall North Common, have been shaped by quarrying and mining. Beyond the reach of modern intensive agriculture, they provide a vital refuge for wildlife, and for Walsall's human inhabitants a much-needed escape from bricks and mortar.

The fourteenth-century walls of Rushall Hall (seen here in an engraving of 1791) are evidence that the local limestone was being quarried for building stone in the medieval period. This superbly preserved but little known scheduled ancient monument saw action in the Civil War when the lady of the manor, Mistress Leigh, 'with the onely helpe of her men and maides', valiantly but unsuccessfully defended the hall from attack by Prince Rupert in 1643. It changed hands again the following year.

Rushall parish has been extensively mined and quarried for both ironstone and limestone. The method of burning lime in pits in Rushall was described at some length in Plot's *Natural History of Staffordshire*, published in 1686. With the opening of the Daw End branch of the Wyrley and Essington Canal around 1800, the lime workings grew in scale. One of the flooded quarries, Park Lime Pits, was landscaped after closure and became a popular beauty spot.

One of Walsall's most attractive areas, the Arboretum, was the scene of extensive limestone quarrying and mining in the eighteenth and nineteenth centuries, linked by tramway to wharves on the Walsall Canal. The workings were prone to flooding and a pumping engine was needed to keep the works dry; when quarrying ceased in the 1840s the workings flooded. In 1874 they reopened as a public park, with the quarries landscaped to form two ornamental lakes.

Part of the former quarry face in the Arboretum, with flooded limestone workings in the foreground, seen in an early twentieth-century postcard. Research has revealed that the water is 60ft deep at this point. Today, at quieter times of the year, the Arboretum serves as a valuable wildlife refuge, and kingfishers and herons can sometimes be seen at this spot, less than a mile from the town centre.

An underground view of the Littleton Street limestone mines in Walsall in about 1900. The mine owner, Louis Lavender, rests his hand on the horse's collar. In the Victorian era limestone was in great demand locally as a flux to help remove impurities in the iron smelting process. The hazards of such working conditions can easily be imagined: Pearce noted in 1813 that 'the falling of the rock is frequently fatal to the miners'.

Opposite above: An early photograph of the Pouk Hill dolerite quarry at Bentley, thought to date from 1875. Dolerite, a form of basalt, is a very hardwearing volcanic rock and its chief use in Walsall was to make chippings for road stone. It is said that the columnar formation of the rocks at Pouk Hill was second only to that of the Giant's Causeway in terms of its geological importance, and the site was regularly visited by Victorian enthusiasts. Sadly, the quarrying was so extensive that little of this feature remained, and the abandoned site was used for landfill.

Opposite below: A detail of the OS map showing Pouk Hill Quarry in 1901. A mineral line can be seen running diagonally from the quarry through a tunnel to wharves on the Anson Branch canal. Wolverhampton Road is at the bottom of the map.

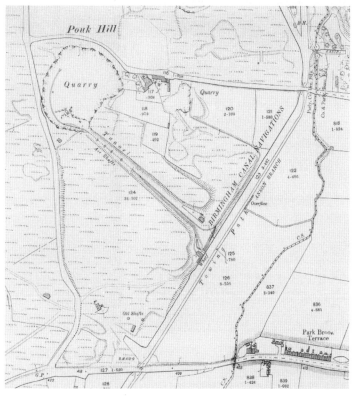

Not a photograph from the Gold Rush, but in fact another view of the Pouk Hill Quarry, where, by the end of the nineteenth century, horse power had been replaced by steam power. A 2ft-gauge steam locomotive was supplied by Bagnalls of Stafford in 1898 and was used to

haul the stone to a canalside crusher, from whence it was loaded directly onto waiting boats. At least half of the men seen here are members of the Handley family.

A Black Country Gin Pit.

Coal mining in Walsall was first recorded in the fourteenth century. As pits became deeper, horse-powered winding 'gins' (short for engines) were erected to help with raising the coal to the surface. In this photograph the winding drum has been placed between two shafts so that as a tub of coal is raised up one shaft, an empty tub is being lowered down the other. The horse can just be seen in the middle of the picture. (Photograph courtesy Ian Bott)

An engraving of 1873 showing miners working the Staffordshire 'thick' coal. The coalfield was famous as one of the richest and most accessible in the country, but by this date much of it had been worked out. It was memorably described in an official report as a 'water-logged rabbit warren'.

Coal mining was always a dangerous occupation. The Pelsall Hall Colliery disaster of November 1872 was one of the worst in the Borough's history. Flood water broke through into the mine, trapping a group of miners underground, and despite valiant rescue efforts twenty-two men and boys were killed. Forty-five children were orphaned. In this contemporary view from *The Illustrated London News*, relatives and neighbours gather to await news.

Walsall Wood Colliery. In its day the deepest colliery on Cannock Chase coalfield (at 1,677ft), it was also the last working pit in Walsall, closing in 1964. It achieved the reputation of being one of the dustiest pits to work in the region. In this view of 1950 a line of tubs, used for hauling the coal underground, can be seen in the foreground, beside a stockpile of ventilation pipes. As recently as the 1950s the pit employed 660 men

QUEEN STREET & PADDOCK
PATENT
BRICK, TILE,
AND
QUARRY WORKS, WALSALL.

HENRY BOYS

Begs to announce that the erection of Machinery for the Manufacture of

PATENT PRESSED BRICKS, TILES, AND QUARRIES

is now complete, and that any quantity may be had by Railway, Canal, or Cart, on the most reasonable terms.

Above: In the nineteenth century numerous small brickworks were active, often worked in conjunction with collieries. Henry Boys' brickworks at Queen Street was one of the largest in Walsall. In this advert of 1885 he announced that, 'the bricks being pressed by steam power... this secures solidity, regularity, and rectangularity of shape...'

A mechanical excavator loading shale onto trucks at the Bentley Hall Brickworks *c.*1950. There were still six brick and tile makers in the Borough in 1922, but during the twentieth century the brick making process became increasingly mechanised, making smaller works uncompetitive.

An aerial view of the Aldridge Brick and Tile Co.'s site in 1934. A colliery was opened here in 1874, with three small brick and tile works operating as subsidiaries. When the colliery closed in 1936 brick and tile production was expanded to 30 million pieces per annum. Among the products were the famous 'Staffordshire Blue' engineering bricks. Extensive rail sidings can be seen between the works and the claypit. (Photograph courtesy Ibstock Brick)

Opposite below: The Henry Boys' Almshouses were erected by the manufacturer in 1887, utilising his own bricks. The almshouses are a fine example of Victorian philanthropy by a wealthy bachelor, and provided housing for twenty-four 'sober and industrious' inmates aged over sixty.

The business was taken over by Ibstock Brick in 1965 and is one of two in Aldridge currently operated by the company, between them producing 1.1 million bricks a week. In this view from around 1960 the kilns can clearly be seen, although the rail sidings seen in the previous image have been removed: road transport had replaced rail! Lichfield Road and the present-day site of the Baron's Court Hotel are at the top of the photograph. (Photograph courtesy Ibstock Brick)

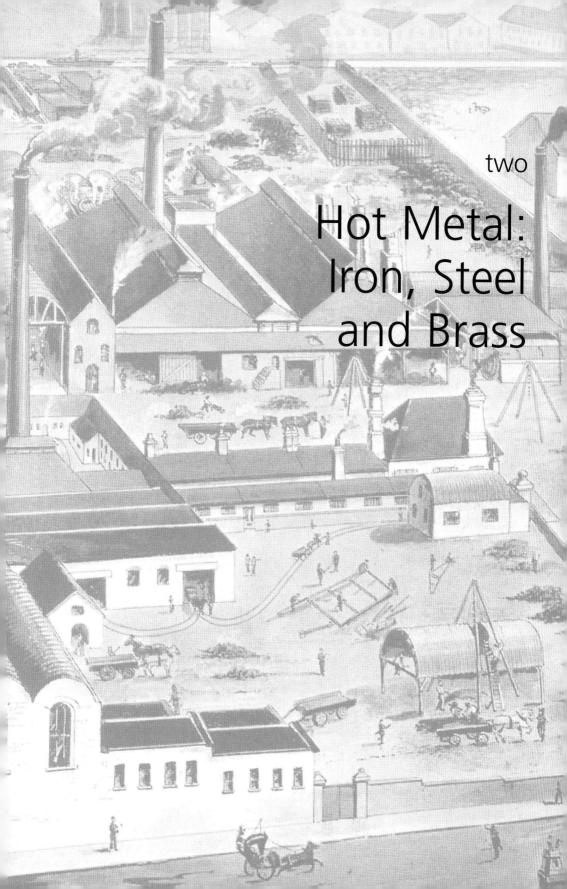

two

Hot Metal: Iron, Steel and Brass

Walsall and metalworking have been inextricably linked for hundreds of years. The origins of the Borough's tradition of metal crafts probably lie in iron working: as we have seen, the local ironstones were being exploited by 1300. By 1450 there were braziers and pewterers active in the Borough as well as ironworkers, and some of the latter were specialising, for example, in making lorinery or small metal items for the horse, such as bits and stirrups. Leland noted 'many smiths and bitmakers' on his visit to Walsall in around 1540. The products made by these craftsmen appear to have been widely distributed. The loriner Richard Hopkes was selling his bits and stirrups as far afield as Devon, Somerset and Yorkshire in 1542. A century later, Walsall's pewterers were equally renowned and a survey of pewter retailers in 1640 found their work being sold in almost every shop in the Midlands, from Hereford to Ashbourne and Northampton to Abingdon. Indeed the leading authorities on the subject have suggested that for a short period, Walsall '... may have been the most important centre of the craft outside London'. During the seventeenth century a variety of other metal crafts was being followed, including bellfounding, nailmaking, brassworking, buckle making, tinning and lockmaking.

Walsall's metalworking tradition was thus distinguished from an early date by two features. Firstly, there was an impressive diversity of trades, and secondly, within the various crafts, a high level of expertise: things produced by Walsall makers were in demand over a wide area. Although the fortunes of the various trades have fluctuated over the centuries, it can be argued that diversity and high levels of skill have been continuing strengths of Walsall's metalworking history, up to and including the present day.

From the late eighteenth century onwards, published directories help to give an impression, albeit incomplete, of Walsall's industrial profile. Sketchley's Directory of 1770 reveals that the 187 buckle and chape makers were the largest single group of metalworkers. By 1813 they had been overtaken by the loriners, whose trade was becoming increasingly international in character. Lorinery remained an important industry throughout the nineteenth century, but it was never dominant, even among the metal trades. A survey of 1866 noted that Walsall's lock industry employed 700, and tube making 1,500, while 3,000 were employed in the Willenhall lock industry, plus an unspecified number in Darlaston's nut and bolt trade. By this date iron casting, especially using malleable iron, was becoming important and in 1896 there were twenty-nine iron foundries across the Borough, producing a variety of items including stoves, street furniture, bicycle parts, builder's ironmongery and 'novelty goods'. In the late nineteenth century engineering gained in importance, with companies such as Rubery Owen producing massive constructions in steel such as entire bridges, a departure from the area's traditional speciality of small items of metal hardware.

As has been noted in the Introduction, metalworking continued to be Walsall's staple trade for most of the twentieth century. For much of the century, trades such as engineering and malleable iron casting did well, and were joined by new crafts such as the making of stainless-steel tableware. By the 1960s, however, there were signs that these trades were losing their competitiveness and were being overtaken by cheaper or more efficient manufacturing overseas. Throughout the Borough, as indeed throughout the West Midlands, there was massive contraction in the metalworking sector from the 1970s onwards. Those metalworking companies that remain in business today are mostly specialists, making innovative and high quality items for niche markets.

Above: Looking across Bourne Pool to the Bourne Vale Pumping Station, Aldridge. We know from documents that an 'iron mill' was in operation here before 1495 when its owner, Simon Montfort, was executed for treason. The Bourne Brook was dammed at this point and the water used to drive a water wheel, which probably powered a tilt hammer, and possibly also bellows. Analysis of excavated material has shown that exceptionally high-grade iron was produced here, probably using iron ore from Rushall. (Photograph courtesy Richard Roberts)

Right: The old treble bell at Worcester Cathedral was cast in 1641 by Thomas Hancox of Walsall. His father, also a bell founder, was Mayor of Walsall in 1620. The Hancox foundry, known as the Pott House, was on the north side of Park Street, backing onto 'the common field of Walsall called the Wisemore'. Hancox bells can be found in churches throughout the Midlands and beyond, and around sixty bells are known to have been cast between 1620–1642. In 1636 the foundry supplied four bells to the church of St Nicholas in Liverpool, which suggests that its reputation was widespread. (Photograph courtesy Richard Roberts)

A detail of Worcester Cathedral's treble bell cast by Thomas Hancox in 1641, with its loyal inscription 'God Save Our King'. The following year the English Civil Wars broke out, and the first major engagement of the wars took place at Powick just outside the city. (Photograph courtesy Richard Roberts)

The Pleck Road area, probably in the late 1920s, with smoke rising from the chimneys of the Alma Tube Works in the foreground. Large ironworks clustered around the banks of the Walsall Canal. They were at their peak in the mid- to late nineteenth century, but by this date many of Walsall's largest ironworks had closed or were in decline, as mild steel replaced wrought and cast iron for many purposes. The Alma Tube Works closed in 1929. Today the name Rollingmill Street and the local pub, the 'Forge Hammer', are reminders of this busy scene.

Nest Common, Pelsall, was the rural setting for one of the area's largest ironworks which in its heyday employed several hundred people, smelting iron ore and making 'bar and sheet iron of the best quality'. Despite its rural location, the Pelsall Ironworks enjoyed excellent supplies of coal from local collieries and good access to the Wyrley and Essington Canal, which meanders across northern Walsall. In this undated but probably mid-Victorian view, the canal crosses the scene from bottom left. The conical blast furnaces would be charged with coke, ironstone and limestone via the steeply sloping ramp or incline on the left of the image.

A group of workers at the Pelsall Ironworks in 1888. A number of tools of the trade can be seen, including pairs of tongs and a ball bogie, held by the man of the left. The latter tool was used to transport balls of red-hot iron between the puddling furnace and the hammer. Working in such hot conditions, it is not surprising that many ironworkers were also said to be heavy drinkers!

A splendid engraving showing one of the Darlaston Steel and Iron Co.'s blast furnaces in 1873. The furnace is the conical tower in the centre of the image. The taller structure in front of it (topped by a flag) is a lift, used to raise the furnace 'charge' with iron ore, limestone and coal. In the foreground, stacks of pig iron await collection by the canalside, and others are being weighed on scales before loading. The Black Country region was still producing 28 per cent of England's pig iron in 1866.

Matthew Harvey & Co. was probably Walsall's largest manufacturer of saddlers' ironmongery, employing 600 people at their Bath Street works in 1914. South America was one of the firm's chief markets. As early as 1858 it was noted: 'bits and spurs are made in large quantities for the South American market; they are of very peculiar construction, of large size and overloaded with ornament…the spurs gilt and with enormous rowels and the stirrups lavishly decorated and of a size and weight that would fairly frighten an English horseman'.

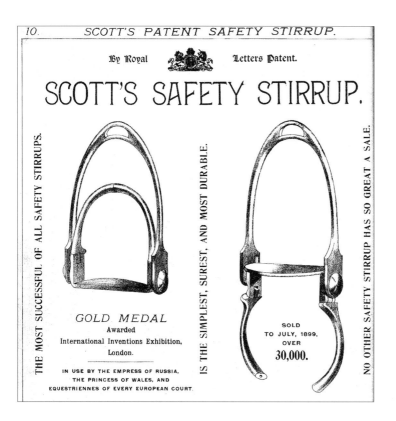

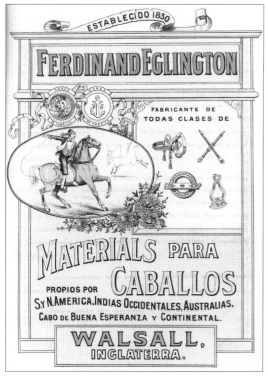

Above: For several centuries Walsall has been the UK's leading centre for the production of stirrups. Of the twenty-seven provincial manufacturers listed in Kelly's Directory of 1889, no fewer than twenty-three were based in Walsall and Bloxwich, and the remaining four in Birmingham. Much ingenuity was invested in coming up with new designs, one of the most successful being Hampson and Scott's safety stirrup, designed to prevent riders being dragged if they should fall. It was supplied to the Empresses of Austria and Russia, and the Princess of Wales.

Left: Ferdinand Eglington of Park Street produced an impressive range of lorinery, much of it for South America. The title page of this catalogue from around 1905 depicts a gaucho with his lasso. The items depicted to the right include a pair of crossed *bombillas* or metal drinking straws, an essential piece of gaucho equipment, also made in Walsall.

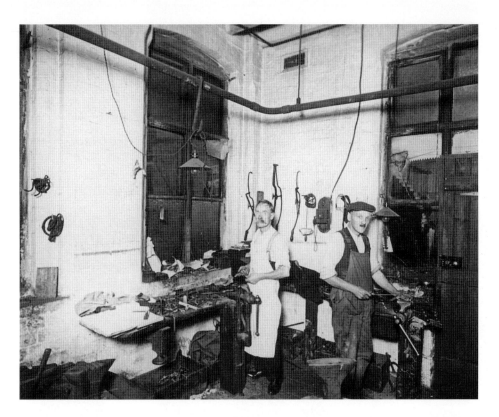

Above: Hand finishing of lorinery was an important part of the process, ensuring that any rough edges or imperfections, which might cause discomfort to horse or rider, were removed. A distinctive tool, the hank and plane, was used to burnish the metal while the item was held securely in a vice. Three examples of this tool can be seen hanging on the wall behind the workmen at Whitehouse Cox in Marsh Street in 1935.

Right: Curry combs, used for grooming horses, were another local speciality. All eight of the UK manufacturers listed in Kelly's Directory for 1889 were based in the Borough, seven of them in Willenhall.

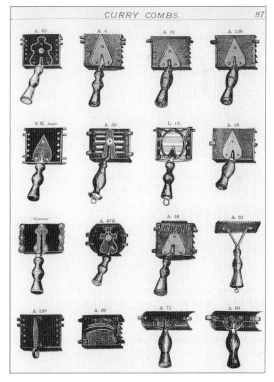

LONDON HANSOM
CAB LAMP.

431

432

435

433

434

REGISTERED H&S TRADE MARK

Lamps for horse-drawn cabs from the *Equine Album* of Hampson and Scott, *c.*1899. Within ten years of this date, demand for such items was falling away, and the more dynamic manufacturers had begun making lamps for the motor trade.

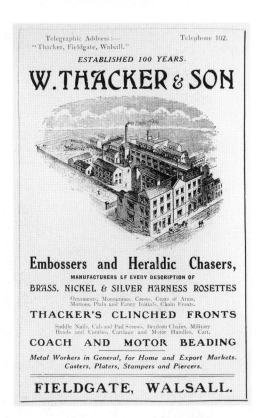

W. Thacker & Son of Fieldgate, near St Matthew's church, specialised in the manufacture of harness furniture. The company is one of only a handful of Walsall lorinery firms to have survived into the twenty-first century.

Buckle making was closely allied to the saddlers' ironmongery trade and, like the latter, was well established in Walsall at an early date, buckle makers being mentioned in the sixteenth century. In 1770 there were no fewer than 278 buckle making workshops in the area. Although some of these specialised in shoe buckles, the majority were probably making buckles for the equine market. Eyland & Sons was one of Walsall's largest buckle makers, absorbing a number of Georgian houses and their gardens in Lower Rushall Street as the business expanded. (Photograph courtesy John Griffiths)

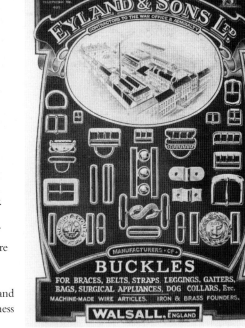

Electroplating buckles at Eyland & Sons, *c.*1900. Electricity revolutionised the laborious job of plating by hand. The workers in the centre of the photograph hold bunches of buckles on strings ready for immersion in the plating tanks. Passing an electrical current through the tanks would result in a layer of metal such as nickel or silver being deposited onto the buckles. (Photograph courtesy John Griffiths)

The wire shop at Eyland & Sons, *c.*1900. The overhead shafting would transmit power from a central engine via belting – often made of leather – to various machinery throughout the site. By this date many Walsall factories used oil or gas engines to drive the machinery. (Photograph courtesy John Griffiths)

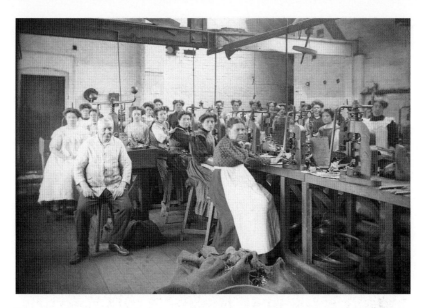

The press shop at Eyland & Sons. A mostly female workforce is using a classic Black Country tool, the fly or hand press, a simple but very effective means of punching out and shaping metal components, achieved with a swing of the press arm. The fly press seems to have been introduced to the area at the end of the eighteenth century. (Photograph courtesy John Griffiths)

Drop forging at Stokes Forgings in Northcote Street. The company was set up in 1908 to make hames and cart gear for working horses. With the decline in this market it successfully moved into making automotive components, and employs some 200 people in this work today. This image from around 1950 shows Gordon Josebury holding a red-hot steel billet in the forge.

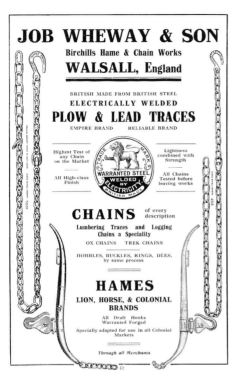

Left: While chain makers in other parts of the Black Country made chain for a variety of purposes, Walsall, as the great manufacturing centre of the Victorian horse world, tended to specialise in producing gear for horse work, such as ploughing and haulage. In this advert from 1916, the 'cart gear' includes a pair of cased hames, so called because the steel case has been wrapped around a central wooden core. The resulting hame was both strong and flexible.

Below: During the Second World War the Bloxwich firm of Wiggin Chains manufactured flailing chains used in the clearing of land mines and barbed wire, seen here in action in 1944. Despite being dismissed as impractical by American commanders, tanks fitted with flailing chains played a crucial role in the D-Day landings, probably saving thousands of lives. (Photograph courtesy Nigel Wiggin)

Casting at an unidentified Walsall foundry, possibly Mathew Harvey and Co. Molten metal is being poured from a crucible into casting boxes, which have previously been prepared with sand to take an impression of the pattern.

The foundry at Josiah Parkes Ltd in Willenhall, c.1930. The man in the centre of the photograph is setting vertical casting boxes or 'flasks' on end ready to receive the molten metal. Two empty crucibles can be seen to the right. The man on the left is stirring the metal, which is being heated in an underground pit furnace. On the right, sand is being prepared ready for more castings – in this case lock parts. (Photograph courtesy Black Country Living Museum)

A loriner hand-finishing a bit at Mathew Harvey and Co., *c.*1979. By this date the traditional methods of hand-forging lorinery had largely died out, and most bits, stirrups and spurs were either stamped or made from cast metal.

John Harper & Co. of Willenhall was one of the largest manufacturers of malleable cast-iron products in the area, employing nearly 700 people at their Albion Works in 1900. Malleable cast iron was introduced to the district in around 1811, and enabled local iron founders to produce castings that were less brittle than those made from traditional cast iron, and capable of being machined.

Opposite above: A number of local companies, including John Harper, manufactured bicycles in the 1890s. The bicycle represented a revolution in mobility for many working class-families, and the sport became hugely popular around this date.

Opposite below: This Vanguard bicycle of 1896, made at the Bradford Street Cycle Works, boasts pneumatic tyres, patented by Dunlop eight years earlier. Within a few years most of the local cycle manufacturers had disappeared, but the making of steel tubing and parts for bicycles continued to be important local industries throughout the twentieth century.

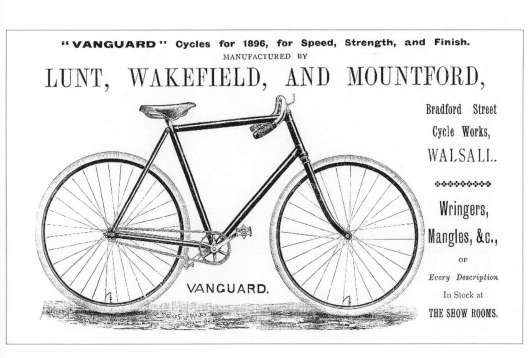

"VANGUARD" Cycles for 1896, for Speed, Strength, and Finish.

MANUFACTURED BY

LUNT, WAKEFIELD, AND MOUNTFORD,

Bradford Street

Cycle Works,

WALSALL.

❖❖❖❖❖❖❖❖❖

Wringers,

Mangles, &c.,

OF

Every Description

In Stock at

THE SHOW ROOMS.

VANGUARD.

Swallow Sidecars was founded by the great William Lyons, best known as the man behind the Jaguar marque. After the Second World War, Swallow was acquired by the firm of Helliwells Ltd, who were based at Walsall Airport. Helliwells went on to produce their own range of scooters.

In 1954 Helliwells launched the celebrated Swallow Doretti sports car. Despite favourable reviews in the motoring press, the company's venture into car manufacturing was short-lived. In his book *Ahead of Time*, R. Cordon Champ suggests that a degree of skullduggery was involved in the Doretti's sudden withdrawal from the market by Helliwells.

In the second half of the nineteenth century, steel increasingly replaced cast iron for engineering purposes. F.H. Lloyd of Darlaston became one of the country's leading manufacturers of heavy steel castings. This view of 1899 shows the melting shop.

The 'heavy foundry' at F.H. Lloyd's James Bridge works in 1899. A contemporary account states that the firm were makers to the British Admiralty, British and foreign railways and tramways, and collieries. Products included wheels, anchors, and ship and engine castings of up to 7 tons in weight.

A group of patternmakers at F.H. Lloyd, *c.*1912. It would have been their responsibility to prepare the wooden patterns used for casting – a highly skilled and exacting task. A pattern for a cog can be seen in the foreground.

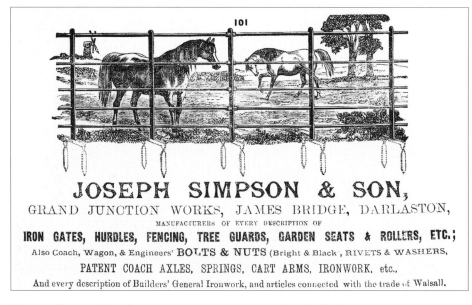

The manufacture of iron fencing and gates became something of a Darlaston speciality in the late nineteenth century. Around the same date the town also became the nut and bolt 'capital' of the UK, with some thirty manufacturers being listed in 1900.

Charles Richards & Sons

Limited.

Contractors to
THE ADMIRALTY,
WAR OFFICE,
INDIA OFFICE.

Crown Agents for
THE COLONIES,
HOME & FOREIGN
RAILWAYS.

Manufacturers of FISH BOLTS & SCREW SPIKES;

also of BRIGHT and BLACK BOLTS and NUTS, RIVETS, WASHERS and GENERAL IRONWORK for Railway Companies, Engineers & Shipbuilders, Motor, Aeroplane & Coach Builders.

Manufacturers of
DROP FORGINGS,
SMITHED FORGINGS,
PRESSINGS, &c.

Makers of THE PATENT IMPERIAL LOCK NUT.
Drawers of BRIGHT HEXAGON and ROUND STEEL.

SPEEDY CUTTING.
QUALITY A SPECIALITY.

Indents through London Merchants.

Imperial Works, DARLASTON, Staffs.

LONDON AGENTS:	AUSTRALIAN AGENT:	NEW ZEALAND AGENTS:
Messrs. C. S. BUCK & CO., Ltd.,	Mr. J. J. MOORE,	Messrs. BUTCHER, REED & CO., Ltd.,
60, Queen Victoria Street,	Lombard Buildings,	39, Lower Taranaki Street,
E.C.	17, Queen Street, MELBOURNE.	WELLINGTON.

Charles Richards & Sons was one of Darlaston's largest nut and bolt manufacturers. Although no longer in operation, the company's former factory in Heath Road is still an impressive landmark.

This bird's eye view of Walker's galvanising works in Pleck Road conveys a sense of the activity and bustle that must have characterised so much of late Victorian Walsall. The firm specialised in galvanised and corrugated iron roofing, but also made iron fencing, nuts and bolts, screws and 'every description of buckets, chamber pails, waterloo coal scoops, foot baths etc.'

One of the most celebrated names in Walsall's history, and in its day one of Britain's largest privately owned industrial concerns, Rubery Owen was founded in 1884 by John Tunner Rubery at the St George's Ironworks in Darlaston. Alfred Ernest Owen joined the enterprise in 1893. The company's original specialities of roofing and bridge construction were soon joined by other products, including iron fencing and gates, nuts and bolts, iron trucks and tanks, and girders and frames of all kinds. This view shows the company's attractive offices in Booth Street, Darlaston. (Photograph courtesy David Owen, Rubery Owen Holdings)

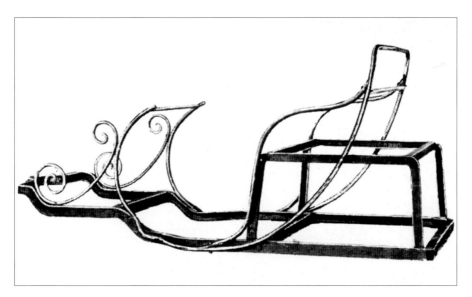

An early Rubery Owen motorcar chassis frame, *c.*1898. Rubery Owen probably achieved greatest fame as a manufacturer of motor components. The company produced its first motorcar chassis in 1896, at the outset of the British motor industry. Rubery Owen was also a pioneer in the aero industry, producing an aviation catalogue as early as 1911 – just three years after the first British powered flight.

A 20-ton girder leaving the company's ironworks at The Green, Darlaston, bound for the Royal School of Music, *c.*1899.

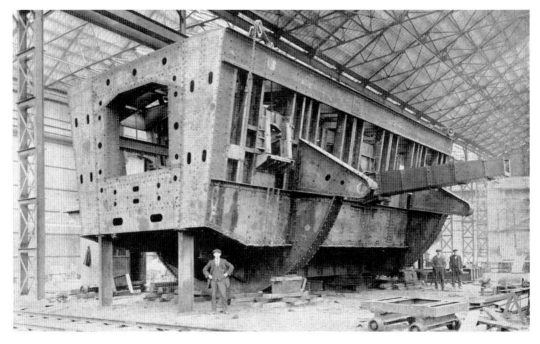

A vast 220-ton steel-framed rolling furnace made by Rubery Owen in 1920. The pouring spout of the furnace can be seen on the right. (Photograph courtesy David Owen, Rubery Owen Holdings)

A view inside the same furnace. Many Darlaston residents can recall the disruption caused by huge steel constructions being manoeuvred through the streets of the town. (Photograph courtesy David Owen, Rubery Owen Holdings)

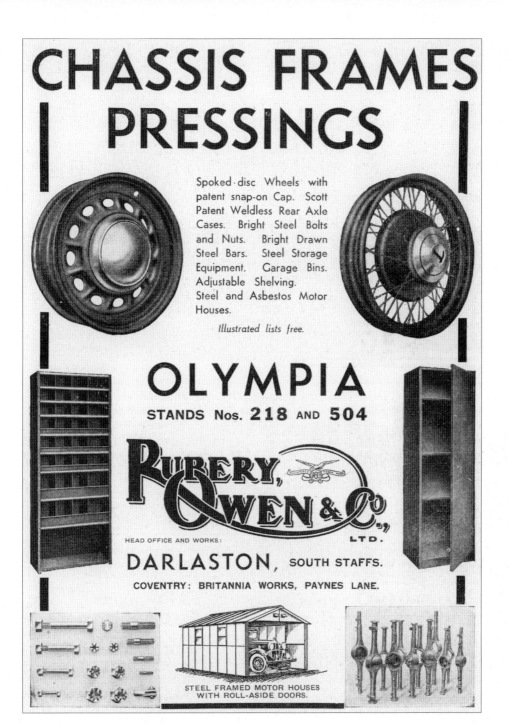

An advertisement from 1936 promoting some of the items which Rubery Owen manufactured and supplied to the motor trade. It has been said: 'strip down every car or truck ever built in Britain before 1980… and you will find a Rubery Owen part somewhere'. A.E. Owen is credited with inventing the pressed steel chassis, a truly revolutionary event that enabled the construction of lighter and therefore faster vehicles.

A footbridge at Bridgnorth constructed by Rubery Owen in 1894, which linked the railway station with High Town. Similar bridges were supplied to railways around the world. The Bridgnorth example was later scrapped, but a replacement has recently been installed to serve the popular Severn Valley Railway. (Photograph courtesy David Owen, Rubery Owen Holdings)

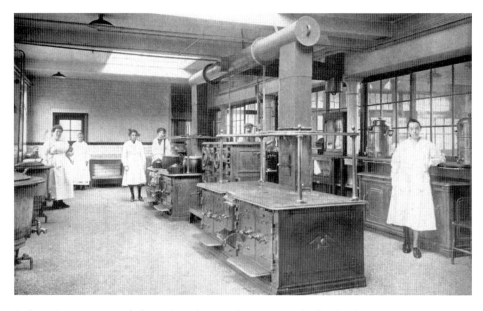

Rubery Owen was an enlightened employer and was among the first local companies to introduce a works canteen, seen here in around c.1920. There were also extensive sports and social facilities for employees. (Photograph courtesy David Owen, Rubery Owen Holdings)

Sir Alfred Owen. Born in 1908, he was thrust into the role of Chief Executive of the company while still a student at Cambridge University, following his father's early death. Under his leadership the Owen organisation became one of the largest industrial conglomerates in the world, incorporating over forty different divisions with a workforce of 16,000. As one of the country's leading suppliers of car components and motor bodies, it was fitting that Sir Alfred should acquire the BRM Formula 1 racing team, which went on to win the World Championship in 1962, with Graham Hill driving. A subsidiary company, Motor Panels Ltd, produced the bodywork for Donald Campbell's world-record-breaking Bluebird in 1963. Sir Alfred died in 1975. (Photograph courtesy David Owen, Rubery Owen Holdings)

During the Second World War Rubery Owen was a major contributor to the war effort. Among the items manufactured by the company were Bailey bridges, wing flaps and tail parts for Stirling and Lancaster bombers, 50-gallon petrol tanks for Spitfires, tank landing craft, parts for the Mulberry harbour, armoured car turrets, steel helmets and 250lb bombs. (Photograph courtesy David Owen, Rubery Owen Holdings)

The current trend in manufacturing in the UK seems to be towards greater specialisation, producing smaller volumes of items of very high quality. L.B. Parkes of Station Street recently finished and anodised the metal discs that clad the dramatic new Selfridges store in Birmingham's Bullring, designed by the Future Projects architectural practice. (Photograph courtesy Stephen Parkes)

three

Old Hall

Somewhat overwhelmed by presents of silver tableware for their twenty-fifth wedding anniversary in 1928, Nellie Wiggin suggested to her husband William that it would save a great deal of polishing if such items could be made from the new 'staybrite' stainless steel. The family firm of J&J Wiggin had recently begun manufacturing bathroom fittings in staybrite, which, although difficult to work, did not corrode or tarnish, and required little or no cleaning. Shortly afterwards, William Wiggin presented his wife with a staybrite toast rack, the world's first (non-cutlery) item of stainless-steel tableware. The world's first stainless-steel teapot followed in 1930, and by 1934 the company was ready to mount an impressive display at the Ideal Home Exhibition, which successfully launched the Old Hall and Staybrite names. For the next fifty years, Old Hall was to be synonymous with stainless-steel tableware.

The Old Hall story had begun in 1893 when father and son, James Thomas and James Enoch Wiggin, commenced hand-forging saddlers' ironmongery in a small converted stable at the rear of their house in Bloxwich. In 1901 they moved to larger premises in Revival Street, a former Salvation Army mission hall known locally as the 'Old Hall'. A busy period making munitions during the First World War was followed by a slump in demand for horse-related products, as the motorcar gained in popularity. In the first of two major changes in direction, the early 1920s saw the company launch a range of bathroom fittings, initially in chrome-plated brass but increasingly in the 18 per cent chromium, 8 per cent nickel quality of stainless steel introduced by Thomas Firth of Sheffield. By the end of the decade Old Hall was the largest manufacturer of stainless-steel bathroom fittings in the country, helped by the inter-war housing boom.

The company's second major departure, thanks to Nellie Wiggin's far-sighted suggestion, was its venture into making stainless-steel tableware. British customers were initially cautious about the new material, not being sure about how hard wearing it would prove to be, but the labour saving advantages of stainless steel over silver and silver plate were undoubtedly a major selling point in an age when servants were becoming increasingly scarce in middle-class households. By 1938 stainless-steel tableware constituted half of the company's turnover, and in the following year exciting new designs were commissioned from the distinguished designer Harold Stabler RDI. War intervened once again, however, and in the years after 1945 government policy pressurised manufacturers to concentrate on export sales to earn desperately needed foreign currency.

Trading conditions improved in the 1950s, and 1955 saw a landmark with the appointment of Robert Welch as consultant designer. The partnership between Old Hall and Robert Welch must rank as one of the twentieth century's happiest collaborations between a designer and a manufacturer, lasting as it did for nearly thirty years and resulting in the creation of icons of twentieth century British design, such as the Campden and Alveston ranges. A recent graduate of the Royal College of Art, Welch agreed to dedicate one day a week producing designs for Old Hall. A steady stream of brilliant and highly original designs followed, which took stainless steel in new directions, both technically and artistically. There was widespread critical acclaim for these designs and Design Council awards resulted in 1958, 1962 and 1965.

Throughout the 1960s Old Hall's success seemed unstoppable. The company's products were being sold in over 2,000 shops in the UK, and there were agents in over twenty countries worldwide. Employees of the period recall that little was kept in stock as products left the factory as fast as they could be made. Old Hall tea sets in particular were in great demand as one of the classic wedding presents of the age, and the millionth teapot was made in 1965. Realising that the company required greater investment to reach its full potential, the Wiggin family sold their interest to Prestige in 1970, and Old Hall looked set for even greater success. The late 1970s, however, saw

A polisher working on teapots from the popular Connaught range, first introduced in 1959. Despite being dirty work, polishing was a highly skilled art. The skills were jealously guarded and it would take many months of training to reach the required standard.

a change in fortune as cheap stainless-steel imports flooded in from the Far East, and Old Hall, whose products were made to a consistently high quality, found it difficult to compete on price. Although Prestige continued to try to develop the company, the dwindling market share resulted in Old Hall being sold again in 1982, to the giant American Oneida cutlery corporation. Two years later the firm was closed – a sad day indeed for Bloxwich and the West Midlands.

Happily, Old Hall's qualities are still appreciated. There are examples of Robert Welch's designs for the company in many major museum collections, including the Victoria and Albert Museum, and the Museum of Modern Art, New York, and a flourishing collector's club, the Old Hall Club, is run by Nigel Wiggin, great-grandson of James Thomas Wiggin.

(All photographs in this chapter are reproduced courtesy of Nigel Wiggin unless otherwise specified.)

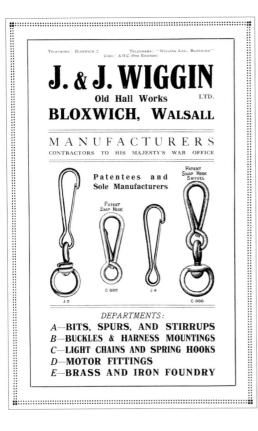

Left: The earliest known advertisement for the company, dating from 1916, four years before the Old Hall brand name was introduced. Saddlers' ironmongery was still the company's main product. (Picture courtesy Walsall Local History Centre)

Below: Part of the firm's Revival Street Works, showing a section of the original 'Old Hall' purchased in 1901 for £160, immediately to the right of the chimney. The building had originally served as a Salvation Army Mission Hall, and was the source of the Old Hall brand name. Over the years the factory expanded to absorb the gardens of a number of nearby houses and it eventually covered nearly three acres.

Above: The founding fathers of the company in 1916. From left to right: Joseph, James Enoch, James Thomas, William, Samuel and Noah Wiggin. The Wiggin family were mostly staunch Methodists and sought inspiration from the Bible when it came to choosing the names of their children!

Below: During the First World War the company, like so many in the Walsall area, concentrated on the production of munitions. This well-populated photograph of 1918 shows only part of the workforce at that date.

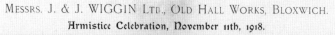

MESSRS. J. & J. WIGGIN LTD., OLD HALL WORKS, BLOXWICH.
Armistice Celebration, November 11th, 1918.

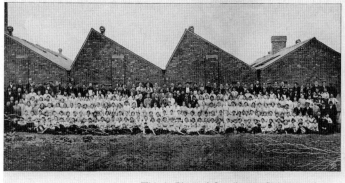

With the Directors' Compliments, Christmas 1918.

Above left: The world's first stainless-steel teapot, made by William Wiggin in 1930, is held here in his right hand by his grandson Nigel's right hand. The early handles were made in erinoid, a type of plastic. Within a few years the company had developed and patented its own stainless steel 'staycool' handles, which proved to be much more satisfactory. Nigel is also holding a later Old Hall teapot, the Alveston, designed by Robert Welch in 1964.

Above right: A page from the first Old Hall catalogue, dated 1932. The toast rack at top right is William Wiggin's original design of 1928, believed to be the world's first item of stainless-steel tableware.

Right: The 'Warwick' tea set was introduced in 1935. It was given a traditional hammered finish to reassure British customers who were still wary of stainless steel. The Warwick name, the first of a long line of castle names given to Old Hall tea services, was intended to convey a sense of strength and grandeur. It was extremely successful and continued in production until 1963.

Below: A rare early Old Hall piece, a stainless steel candleholder with a decidedly 'Art Deco' look. This design appeared in the 1936 catalogue but had been withdrawn by the following year. (Private collection)

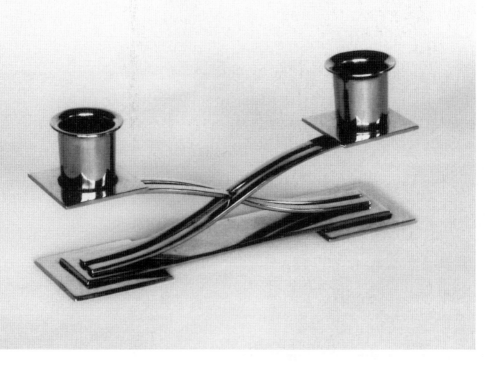

Left: The 'Cottage' tea service, introduced in 1938. In the official registration papers the design is credited to William Wiggin's wife Nellie, though this was probably a case of family loyalty!

Below: A J&J Wiggin team of employees and management, proud winners of the Bloxwich Cricket Club Knockout Cup, *c.*1948. Back row, extreme right, Noah Wiggin, with Philip Robinson, works director, beside him. Front row, from left to right: Oscar Dunn, Leslie Wiggin, Charlie Buffery, Les Jones, -?-.

A Pickfords lorry lowering part of a 160-ton press into the factory in the mid-1950s. The sheer bulk of such presses meant that they could only enter the building via the roof.

IDEAL HOME AUGUST 1958

"What
a lovely
teaset
Joan!"

EVERYONE ADMIRES JOAN. She *knows* about good design. The latest thing to earn compliments for her is this new Heirloom Teaset.

Made to last a lifetime, it's wonderfully easy to keep clean. *And the teapot actually makes tea go further.*

STAINLESS STEEL	TEAPOT	48/-
	SUGAR BOWL	15/1
	CREAM JUG	27/2
	TRAY	56/6

Send for free leaflet and name of your stockist to

J. & J. WIGGIN LTD., 2 OLD HALL WORKS, BLOXWICH, WALSALL, STAFFS

WT56A

Above: Old Hall staff enjoying their annual dinner dance at Bloxwich Baths, *c.*1955. Samuel Wiggin is in the centre of the photo, third row from the front, with fellow directors Noah and John Wiggin on his left and Leslie Wiggin on his right.

Left: An advertisement from 1958. Robert Welch advised the company to drop the 'e' in 'Olde' as he felt it gave an old-fashioned image that was out of step with the times. From 1959 onwards, all of the company's products were marked Old Hall.

Right: The 'Cumberland' was one of the company's most popular tea sets, and sold especially well to the catering trade. It is still to be found in daily use in many homes in Walsall – including the author's.

Below: Robert Welch, seen on the far right, with John and Leslie Wiggin on the left, are celebrating winning their first Design Council Award in 1958, for the Campden toast rack. Old Hall was to win a further two such awards, in 1962 and 1965.

One of Robert Welch's most celebrated designs for Old Hall, the Alveston tea set, was introduced in 1964. The teapot was a technical masterpiece. The spout was cast using the 'lost wax' process (which gave a very smooth finish), and was then welded to the main body, which was formed in a power press. Relatively few Alveston teapots were made as the work involved meant that they were always expensive to produce.

Old Hall commissioned Robert Welch to design the Alveston cutlery range in 1963. It was instantly recognised as a classic, becoming another Design Award winner for the company in 1965. Alveston was the name of the attractive village near Stratford-on-Avon where Robert Welch lived.

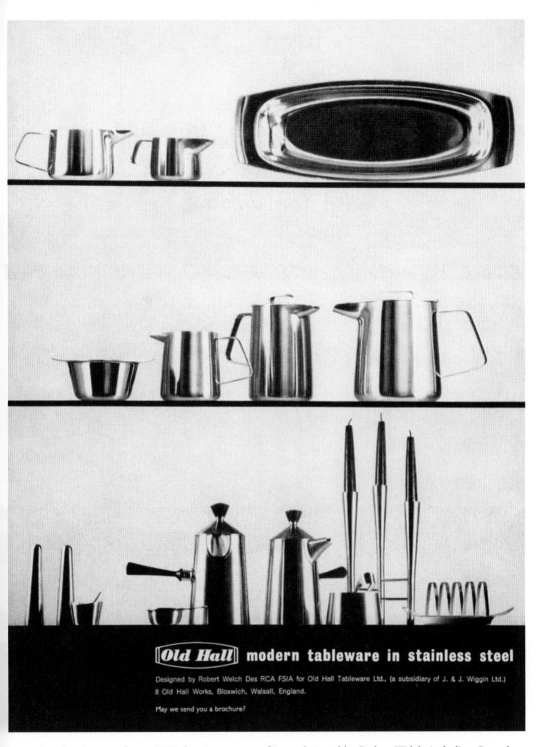

Old Hall modern tableware in stainless steel

Designed by Robert Welch Des RCA FSIA for Old Hall Tableware Ltd., (a subsidiary of J. & J. Wiggin Ltd.)
8 Old Hall Works, Bloxwich, Walsall, England.

May we send you a brochure?

An advertisement from *c.*1963 showing a range of items designed by Robert Welch, including Campden coffee pots and Oriana jugs. The latter were commissioned by the P&O shipping line for use on board their new luxury liner, the *Oriana.* This was the largest commission in Old Hall's history.

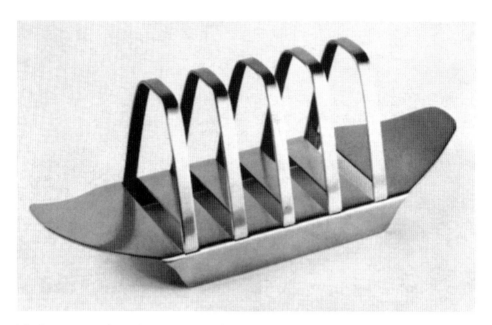

The Design Council award-winning Campden toast rack, designed by Robert Welch for Old Hall in 1957. It was available in two-, four-, and six-slice versions.

The Campden condiment set designed by Robert Welch in 1957; a special grade of extra-corrosion-resistant steel was used for condiment sets.

The Alveston condiment set by Robert Welch, designed in 1962 and a real contrast to the set in the previous photograph, although only five years separate them.

A general view of one of the polishing shops. Toast racks can be seen on the shelves in the foreground. Note the fume extraction hoods behind the polishing wheels.

Left: Heavy power presses are an essential tool in shaping stainless steel, which is an exceptionally difficult material to work. Stainless steel 'work hardens', which means that it needs to be repeatedly annealed (alternately heated and cooled) at approximately 1,100°C. A relatively tall shape like a hot water jug, for example, might have to be returned to the press three or four times before the desired shape could be achieved.

Below: Part of the reduced workforce in 1978 celebrates the fiftieth anniversary of Old Hall's production of the world's first stainless-steel toast rack. Cheap imports had made large inroads into the company's markets by this date, and final closure came in 1984.

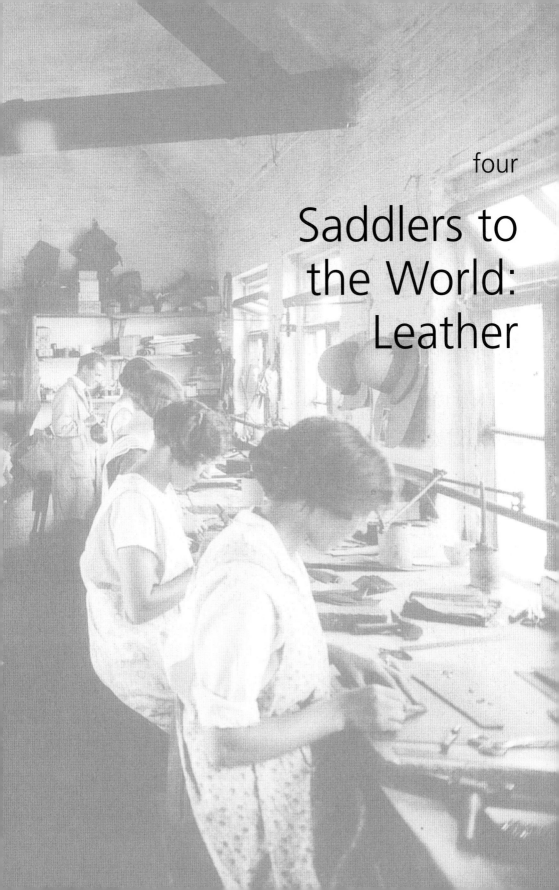

four

Saddlers to the World: Leather

'Walsall… the chief seat of saddlery manufacture in the kingdom.'
(William Franklin, *The Walsall Trades*, 1866)

The growth of the Walsall leather trade was largely a nineteenth-century phenomenon. Although there had been a tannery in the town in the fifteenth century, as late as 1801 there were fewer than thirty leatherworkers producing horse equipment in Walsall, of whom just four were saddlers. In the following decades a number of local producers of saddlers' ironmongery began to experiment with producing bridles, saddlery and harnesses, and to distribute these products over a wide area. These initial ventures seem to have met with success and from 1850 onwards growth in Walsall's leather trade was dramatic, helped by booming demand for saddlery and harnesses, an expanding rail network and growing British power and influence overseas. One local saddler, Thomas Newton, proudly entitled his catalogue 'The Saddlery of All Nations', an accurate reflection of the boundless commercial ambitions of the town's Victorian manufacturers. By the 1870s demand was such that the more successful saddlery and harness manufacturers began to build imposing three-storey factories, bringing workers who had previously worked from home under one roof. The largest factories, such as that of John Leckie and Co., could accommodate up to 300 workers.

In 1900, at the peak of the trades, Walsall had almost 150 saddlery and harness manufacturers, employing over 6,800 men and women, nearly a quarter of the national total. Another thousand or so people worked in tanning and currying leather. Walsall manufacturers dominated the ready-made saddlery and harness trade of late Victorian Britain, and produced an astonishing variety of other horse-related wares, from carriage lamps to curry combs and May Day decorations, making it the great international emporium for horse goods. Walsall firms also took a large share of the export trade, with important markets in Australia, South Africa, and North and South America.

Most of the images in this chapter date from this 'Golden Age', although it should be remembered that for many of those working in the trade, a fifty- to sixty-hour working week was normal. Women stitchers would be lucky to take home ten shillings a week, about a third of the wage of a master saddler, and if some of the work called for real skill and judgment, much of it must have been highly repetitive and even physically exhausting. A Walsall saddler wrote in 1890 that the work required 'every nerve to be strained, and muscle too in some jobs such as finishing… it is very common for men continually at this job to be compelled to stop work on account of their wrists swelling'. In the tanning and currying trades, hernias and ruptures were common injuries, caused by the strain of moving bundles of wet hides, often up and down staircases as steep as ladders.

The twentieth-century images included here show that with the coming of the motorcar, many of the town's saddlers and harnessmakers reinvented themselves as makers of light leather goods, producing items such as purses, bags and wallets. By 1931, one in every six women employed in Walsall was engaged in such work. Though the saddlery and harness trade continued to decline between the wars, the success of the light or 'fancy' leather trade kept a wealth of leatherworking skills alive in the town.

The growth in riding for pleasure as a popular recreation in the 1960s brought about an upsurge in demand for saddles and other horse equipment. As a new generation of apprentices completed their training, many of them went on to establish their own workshops, and the number of businesses multiplied. While in recent years the light leather goods industry has shrunk, and gloving and tanning have disappeared from the town altogether, saddlery has been one of Walsall's great post-war success stories. With some seventy manufacturers currently based in the town, exporting an estimated three-quarters of their output, Walsall is generally considered to be the greatest saddle-making town in the world.

(All photographs in this chapter are from the collection of Walsall Leather Museum, Walsall Museums Service, unless otherwise stated.)

Sir E.T. Holden was one of the great figures of the Walsall leather trade. He inherited his father's business when he was just nineteen and steadily developed its reputation for high-quality leather, in particular pigskins and japanned or patent leather. He was three times the Mayor of Walsall, and was elected MP for the town in 1891. He never liked motorcars, and right up to his death at the age of ninety-five in 1926, he insisted on coming to work in a horse-drawn brougham. Ironically, another branch of the family emigrated and founded Australia's best-known car manufacturer, Holden Motors.

Founded in 1819, E.T. Holden & Sons was probably Walsall's largest Victorian tannery, employing over 100 people in 1881. The site was presumably chosen for its proximity to the Walsall Brook, which can be seen emerging from a culvert in the foreground of this engraving of 1894. Later, the very narrow access from Park Street caused serious problems, and the firm relocated in 1967, the site then being redeveloped for the Saddler's Shopping Centre.

Right: The Whittimere Street site of Handford Greatrex & Brother was probably Walsall's oldest tannery site, in continuous use for 300 years until its closure in 1970. In this view of 1893, open tanning pits can be seen in the furthest yard, and in the foreground a wagon is shown in front of the bark store, which could hold 1,000 tons of oak bark when full.

Below: The covered tan yard at Handford Greatrex in 1895. Skins and hides would be continually moved between the pits, which were filled with varying strengths of 'liquor', a solution of ground oak bark, until the hides were fully tanned. The whole process at Handford Greatrex took up to thirteen months, after which the hides were then ready for currying.

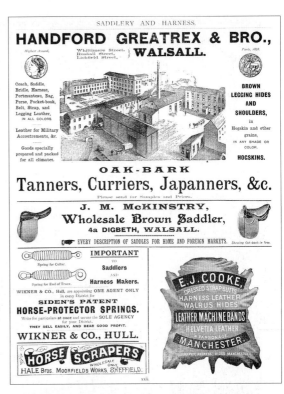

Japanned or patent leather was in great demand in the nineteenth century for making showy sets of harnesses. The leather was first nailed to a board and then coated with layers of linseed oil and indigo, which would be baked in an oven until set, and then polished smooth with pumice stone. This process would be repeated between six and twelve times until the required finish was achieved. The japanners, as here, usually worked stripped to the waist to ensure that no dust or fibres from their clothing could drop onto the linseed oil and spoil the finish.

The scouring shop at Handford Greatrex in 1895. Scouring involved working the wet hides to remove any surface bloom resulting from the tanning process.

ANTHRAX.

Common Appearance of Anthrax on the Skin.

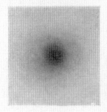 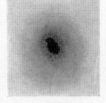 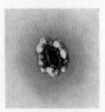

On 1st or 2nd day.   On 3rd or 4th day.   Later Stage.

ANTHRAX is a fatal disease affecting certain animals, which may be conveyed from them to man — especially to those handling hides, wool or horsehair of animals which have died of the disease. Occasionally also Anthrax in man has been traced to the unloading of other cargoes, such as grain.

A sign warning tanners of the danger of anthrax, dated 1906. Cases of anthrax were extremely rare, and the chief occupational hazard for tanners and curriers in Walsall was injury caused by lifting piles of hides. Hernias were commonplace.

The shaving shop at Handford Greatrex in 1895. Shaving was done by hand using a two-handled knife and was a highly skilled process. A contemporary noted: 'Shaving is the most delicate part of the currier's work, for should he by mischance take too much off or cut a hole in the leather it is more or less ruined.'

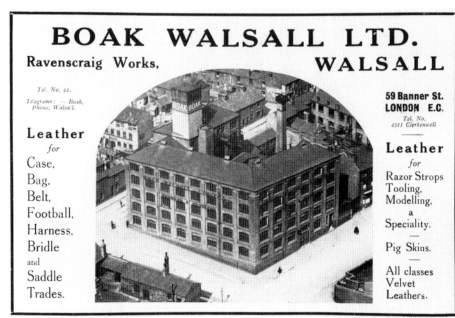

BOAK WALSALL LTD.

Ravenscraig Works,　　　　　　　　WALSALL

Tel. No. 44.

Telegrams: — Boak,
Phone, Walsa'l.

59 Banner St.
LONDON E.C.
Tel. No.
4511 Clerkenwell

Leather
for
Case,
Bag,
Belt,
Football,
Harness,
Bridle
and
Saddle
Trades.

Leather
for
Razor Strops
Tooling,
Modelling,
a
Speciality.

Pig Skins.

All classes
Velvet
Leathers.

Say you saw the Advertisement in " Leather Goods."

Above: 'The Boak' is probably the best-known landmark of Walsall's leather trade, dominating the Leather Quarter. Established in 1903 by a group of Scottish industrialists, the firm was best known for the production of pigskins. The water tower was added in 1917, presumably to enable the firm to cope with the massive increase in demand for military saddlery and leather accoutrements during the First World War.

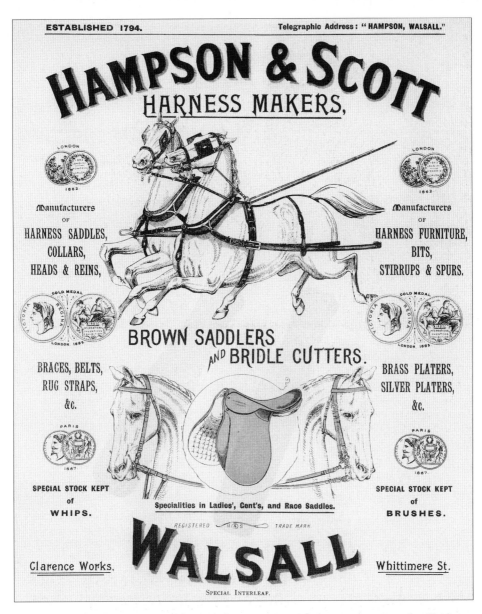

ESTABLISHED 1794.

Telegraphic Address: "HAMPSON, WALSALL."

HAMPSON & SCOTT
HARNESS MAKERS,

Manufacturers
OF
HARNESS SADDLES,
COLLARS,
HEADS & REINS,

Manufacturers
OF
HARNESS FURNITURE,
BITS,
STIRRUPS & SPURS.

BROWN SADDLERS
AND BRIDLE CUTTERS.

BRACES, BELTS,
RUG STRAPS,
&c.

BRASS PLATERS,
SILVER PLATERS,
&c.

SPECIAL STOCK KEPT
of
WHIPS.

Specialities in Ladies', Gent's, and Race Saddles.

SPECIAL STOCK KEPT
of
BRUSHES.

REGISTERED   H&S   TRADE MARK

WALSALL

Clarence Works.

Whittimere St.

SPECIAL INTERLEAF.

Hampson & Scott was one of Walsall's great success stories. Originating as a maker of saddlers' ironmongery, the firm diversified into making or wholesaling a huge range of products for the horse world. Their splendid 'Equine Album' is one of the most comprehensive catalogues of horse-related items ever produced.

Opposite below: An unusual bird's eye view of Walsall town centre, looking towards St Matthew's Church in about 1905. The London Saddlery Works of John Leckie & Co. is conspicuous in Goodall Street. The other half of this substantial building was occupied by Brace Windle, Blyth, & Co., saddlers and export merchants, and to its right is the saddlery and harness factory of Overton & Co. Church Hill is still crowded with tall eighteenth- and early nineteenth-century houses at this date.

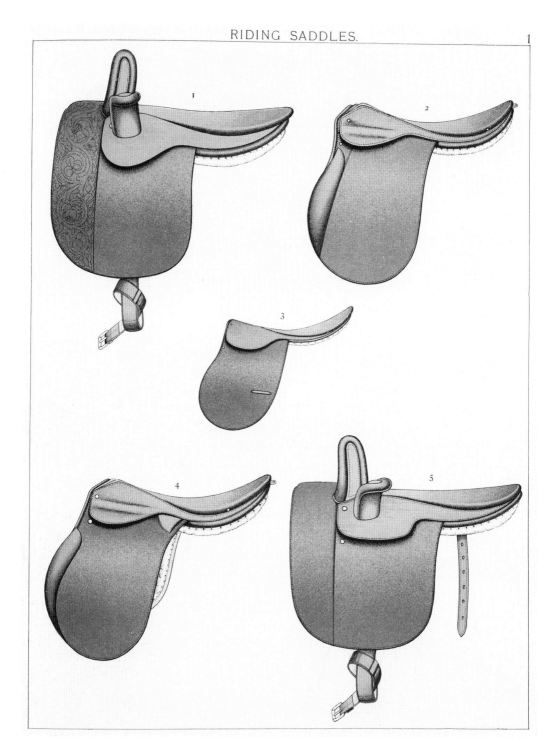

A variety of saddles from E.J. Parkes' catalogue of 1902. They include side saddles, a race saddle (No.3) and a gentleman's full shafto, the latter priced at around £4. This would have represented at least two weeks' wages for a highly skilled saddler of the period.

Hampson & Scott erected splendid new premises, the Clarence Works, in Whittimere Street in 1891. Sadly, these were demolished in 1988 to make space for a supermarket.

Bits, stirrups and spurs are being sorted and packed in this view of Hampson & Scott's warehouse in about 1895. Horse collars hang from above.

Making military riding saddles at Messrs Moss Stone, Butts Road, in the early 1920s. Excellent natural light fills the workshop, but perhaps the most striking thing to modern eyes is the lack of space that each saddler occupies. (Photograph courtesy Graham Evans)

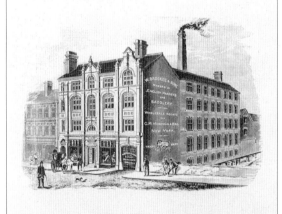

C. M. MOSEMAN & BROTHER, NEW YORK.

MANUFACTURING ESTABLISHMENT OF C. M. MOSEMAN & BROTHER.

WALSALL, NEAR LONDON, ENGLAND.

Makers of High Class Saddles, Bridles, etc. for the Hunt, the Race, Steeplechase, Polo Playing,
the Park, Road and School.

Also, Harness for Four-in-Hand, Tandem, Pair or Single Horse Traps, Broughams, Cabs, etc.

Horse Clothing, Rugs, Rollers, Muzzles, etc., and, in fact,

Everything for the Complete Equipment of a First Class Establishment.

Above: Saddle trees are an essential component of most saddles, forming the (usually concealed) wood and metal framework. The firm of Beebee & Beebee was located in Wednesbury Road before relocating to Lower Forster Street, where it still operates today. In this view of around 1930 Tom Hateley is third from right, with his father Henry standing behind him. Tom later became foreman of the factory. (Photograph courtesy Pat Andrews)

Left: W. Brookes & Son was another of Walsall's pioneering saddlery and harness firms. Having originated as a saddlers' ironmongers, the firm began making bridles in about 1830. With the opening of a railway station at Bescot, about two miles from the town centre, in 1837, exports became an important element of the Walsall trade, which they have remained ever since. Brookes specialised in production for the North American market, though this illustration suggests that their American partners had a somewhat sketchy idea of British geography!

Right: With such highly developed leatherworking skills it is not surprising that the town's craftsmen and women should turn their hands to making more than saddlery and harnesses. A pocket-book maker, William Granger, is recorded in 1841, and by 1900 there were few leather items not being made somewhere in the town. The bags shown here in an Overton & Co. catalogue from around 1900 include a kit bag (745a), a true Gladstone bag (745), a hat box (748) and a Saratoga trunk (2509).

Below: Saddle tree making at Moss Stone & Co. in the early 1920s. The tree parts were shaped from blocks of beech wood, using drawshaves and rasps. Completed trees hang from the ceiling, and piles of shavings litter the workshop. Four of the men wear chest protectors to prevent injury while shaving the wood. There are currently ten saddle tree makers in Walsall, probably the greatest concentration in the world. (Photograph courtesy Graham Evans)

PORTMANTEAUS, BAGS, &c.   87

DO NOT CUT THE BOOK
In ordering it is only necessary to quote the number

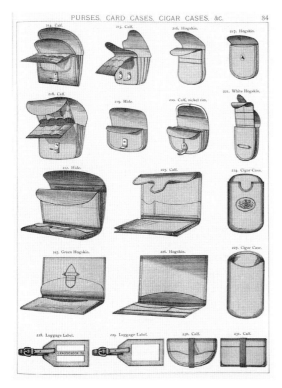

Left: Typical fancy or light leather goods of the Edwardian period. The coming of the motorcar meant there was a declining demand for horse equipment after 1905, and Walsall was fortunate that the light leather goods trade could take up at least some of the slack.

Below: The fancy leather cutting room at Moss Stone. Cutters, who were nearly always male, were considered the elite of the fancy leather trade, and were certainly among the best-paid workers. Using clicking knives they would carefully cut around patterns placed on the leather to produce the various components. Much skill was called for in achieving the maximum number of usable components from each skin or hide. (Photograph courtesy Graham Evans)

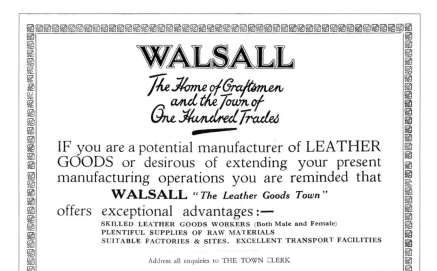

WALSALL
The Home of Craftsmen and the Town of One Hundred Trades

IF you are a potential manufacturer of LEATHER GOODS or desirous of extending your present manufacturing operations you are reminded that

WALSALL *"The Leather Goods Town"*

offers exceptional advantages :—

SKILLED LEATHER GOODS WORKERS (Both Male and Female)
PLENTIFUL SUPPLIES OF RAW MATERIALS
SUITABLE FACTORIES & SITES. EXCELLENT TRANSPORT FACILITIES

Address all enquiries to THE TOWN CLERK

In this advertisement of 1929, placed by Walsall Borough Council, no mention is made of the struggling saddlery trade. The future is seen to lie with the growing light leather goods trade and rightly, the town's primary competitive advantage is seen as its skilled workforce. The number of light leather goods manufacturers had grown to about ninety by this date, between them employing around 3,000 people.

The fancy leather workshop at Moss Stone, *c.*1920–25. Women are busy assembling the previously cut pieces of leather. The woman in the centre of the photo is using a heated bevel to mark the edge of the item with a decorative 'tramline'. Adjustable gas jets for heating the bevels can be seen projecting from the walls. (Photograph courtesy Graham Evans)

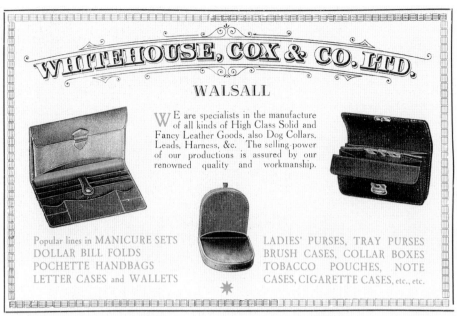

Like so many of Walsall's leather manufacturers, Whitehouse Cox originated as saddlers' ironmongers. By the date of this advert, 1929, they were primarily making fancy leather goods. The company has recently moved to Aldridge, and continues to make high-quality leather goods, mostly for export to Japan and the United States.

Fancy leather goods being made at Whitehouse Cox, *c.*1930. (Photograph courtesy Mrs Pauline Brown)

The 'Turned Edge' shop at Moss Stone, *c*.1920–25. Turned edge work was considered to be of superior quality to cut edge work since great skill was required in paring or skiving the leather thin enough for it to be turned back on itself. The finished goods were considered to be more durable and generally commanded a higher price. Turned edge workshops had their own characteristic noise, as the women hammered then glued the edges and corners of the leather flat. (Photograph courtesy Graham Evans)

The Mark Cross workforce outside the factory in Warewell Street in 1936. The company was famous for its leather goods, most of which were exported to the United States where the company had a store on Fifth Avenue, New York. Joan Waltho, who started work there in 1934, remembers the superb craftsmanship of the older workers, as well as the ramshackle working conditions. Joan is standing in the middle with her prized Hercules bicycle, which she bought in weekly instalments of 2*s* 3*d*. (Photograph courtesy Mrs Joan Waltho)

Left: Frank Ringrose in his saddlery workshop, Midland Road, in 1952. Frank was eighty-eight at the time of this photograph. He is still remembered in the town as a superb craftsman. (Photograph courtesy Graham Evans)

Below: The shaving team at Handford Greatrex tannery, *c.*1961. By this date all shaving of leather was done on a large machine. From left to right: Walter Horobin, Les Williams, Geoff Crowe, Graham Ward, Tom Proffitt, Terry Hope, Stan -?-, unknown lad in foreground. (Photograph courtesy Geoff Crowe)

Leon Jessel came to Walsall as a refugee from Nazi Germany. After a period of internment on the Isle of Man he settled in Walsall, establishing a company making high-quality leather goods. Leon Jessel's Camden Street Factory was built by Sheldon & Sons in 1872 and was described by the *Walsall Observer* in a contemporary account as probably the largest bridle factory in the world.

Using a flatbed clicking press to cut out leather goods components at Leon Jessel Ltd, *c.*1980. Steel 'knives' are placed face down on the leather and the arm of the press is swung into position; as the two buttons on the arm are depressed it drops onto the knife, cutting out the leather beneath.

Florence Walker, hand-stitching a girth at Jabez Cliff in 1973. Widowed at an early age, she raised four children single-handedly, stitching the famous 'Cliff' brand leather footballs to earn a living. When this trade declined she turned her hand to bridle stitching. Jabez Cliff continues to trade worldwide and the company is Royal Warrant Holder for saddlery and lorinery to HM The Queen. (Photograph courtesy Mr Grimley, copyright *Walsall Observer*)

five

Locks and
Keys

'Willenhall, the real seat of the lock, door-bolt and latch manufacturers for the world…'
(Samuel Griffiths, *Guide to the Iron Trade*, 1873)

The Black Country is remarkable for its highly localised concentrations of particular trades. Midway between Walsall and Wolverhampton, yet quite distinct from both, is the small town of Willenhall, the centre of the British lock trade, and an outstanding example of what has been termed 'localised industrial specialisation'.

Lock making has a long history in the area, but in the seventeenth century it was Wolverhampton rather than Willenhall that was considered to be the main centre of this trade. Willenhall seems to have overtaken its neighbour around the middle of the eighteenth century. Dr Wilkes, a local resident, reckoned that two-fifths of the town's 250 houses were occupied by locksmiths in 1760, and ten years later a total of 148 locksmiths were listed under Willenhall, compared with 134 for Wolverhampton. Most of these businesses would probably have been very small, consisting of a single-storey backyard workshop with a forge, stocked with hand tools such as hammers, files, shears, bellows, punches and leg vices. A typical 'little master' of the period would have employed no more than half a dozen journeymen and apprentices, many of whom would eventually establish their own workshop. The industry continued to expand throughout the first half of the nineteenth century, so that by 1855 there were 340 workshops in the town, supplying foreign as well as British markets.

It is clear from contemporary accounts that the intense competition for work created by so many small workshops led to appalling conditions in the trade. A seventy-hour working week was quite normal, and often exceeded, and there was a heavy reliance on the labour of children and young apprentices, many of them recruited from the workhouse. The Children's Employment Commission of 1843 found that children as young as seven would be 'put to the vice' as soon as they could hold a file. The long hours spent filing locks from an early age resulted in many locksmiths becoming physically deformed, with one shoulder permanently higher than the other, and the left leg bent inwards at the knee, and it was said that a Willenhall man could be identified by his gait. The Commission's report paints a picture of a violent and lawless society, with apprentices – of whom there were over 600 in Willenhall and Wednesfield – being regularly beaten by drunken masters, and with many people living in utter poverty and filth. Typhus was endemic. Disraeli undoubtedly used this report as a source for his novel *Sybil*, in which he portrayed Willenhall as Wodgate, 'the ugliest spot in England… a vast squalid suburb', and four years later, in 1849, the town was visited by cholera, leaving 292 people dead. The churchyard was so full that an emergency burial ground had to be opened nearby.

From this low point conditions began to improve. A literary institute was opened in 1864 containing a library, lecture hall and classrooms, and membership of friendly societies became the norm amongst locksmiths. A lockmakers' union was formed in 1889 to fight for better pay and working conditions. New and spacious streets of terraced housing were laid out around the old core of the town, served by piped water and drainage. By the end of Victoria's reign the town possessed over twenty nonconformist chapels, a dramatic change from earlier in the century when, as Samuel Griffiths recalled, there was 'one church, with a blaspheming drunken parson, who spent six times more time in the public house than the church'. Disraeli's Wodgate had been transformed, and for much of the community self-improvement and sobriety were now the order of the day.

In the early twentieth century the shift from workshop to factory, which had begun some years earlier, gathered pace. The traditional hand tools of the lockmaker, such as the anvil, hammer and vice, were still in evidence, but the larger firms, such as Josiah Parkes, H. & T. Vaughan, and

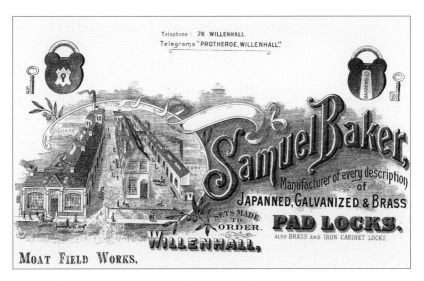

Telephone : 76 WILLENHALL.
Telegrams "PROTHEROE, WILLENHALL".

Samuel Baker,
Manufacturer of every description of
JAPANNED, GALVANIZED & BRASS
PAD LOCKS.
SETS MADE TO ORDER.
ALSO BRASS AND IRON CABINET LOCKS.
WILLENHALL,
MOAT FIELD WORKS,

In the late nineteenth century the fields to the north of the town centre were laid out with new streets, and the area was developed with purpose-built lock factories. Samuel Baker's factory was built in Moat Street in 1884. In these new factories steam power was used to drive equipment such as presses and bobbing and polishing machines, and the various tasks involved in lock production were divided between separate workshops, each with its own foreman. (Collection of Walsall Museums)

E. Tonks & Sons invested heavily in banks of machinery such as capstan lathes, heavy power presses, vertical drilling machines, and bobbing and polishing machines, all driven by a central power source. The master locksmith was still required to assemble the locks from castings and pressings, and to develop prototypes, but much of the production and assembly work was now done by women, especially in the production of the cylinder or 'yale' lock, an American invention that became increasingly important to the trade after 1900. Although women had worked in the lock trade for many years, this process was accelerated by the First World War, and the local locksmiths' union, which had opposed membership for women, finally gave way in 1916. As can be seen from the photographs reproduced here, women outnumbered men in many of the factories, undertaking a wide range of work including lock assembly, polishing, lacquering and packing.

Willenhall firms dominated the production of mass-produced locks in the UK for most of the twentieth century, and as recently as 1962 it was estimated that the town and its immediate neighbourhood produced 90 per cent of the country's locks. Since then the industry has seen a spate of takeovers, mergers and closures in response to intense competition from low-wage manufacturing in the Far East. Today, approximately 50 per cent of locks sold in this country are imported. Several of the most famous names in the industry, including Josiah Parkes, Yale and Chubb Locks, are now part of one large (Swedish-owned) combine. It would, however, be wrong to assume that the small independent lock manufacturer is entirely a figure of history, and a visitor to the town can still find a number of specialist manufacturers tucked away in side streets, sometimes in the same buildings that they have occupied for over a century. One of the finest surviving examples of a Victorian lockmaker's workshop, in New Road, is now open to the public as 'The Locksmith's House', a branch of The Black Country Living Museum.

(All photographs in this chapter are courtesy of The Black Country Living Museum, unless otherwise specified.)

Above: The bobbing and machine shops at E. Tonks & Sons' works at Temple Bar, *c.*1900. Bobbing has been defined as: 'a preparatory or finishing process given to an article by holding it against a wheel of felt for example… which revolves at high speed'. Polishing involves rapidly rotating cloth or leather mops charged with a fine abrasive compound. The women machinists appear to be drilling holes in lock cases. (Collection of Walsall Museums)

Opposite below: The machine and press shop at Josiah Parkes in 1914. The First World War brought large numbers of women into the lock factories to help with munitions production. Nearly 700 women joined the lockmakers' union in 1916. In contrast to photographs from the 1920s, the women are not wearing caps to protect their hair, despite the threat posed by the unguarded machinery belting.

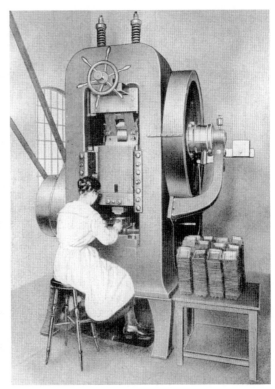

Right: Operating a 400-ton machine press during the First World War at H. & T. Vaughan. It has been said: 'the most useful machine tool in the trade is a press... almost anything can be done to sheet metal in a press equipped with the right tools'.

Below: Assembling hand grenades at H.&T. Vaughan in Willenhall during the First World War. Working conditions were not easy for the women. They were not generally permitted to talk at work and seem to have been viewed by some male workers as a threat to their jobs. (Collection of Walsall Museums).

No. 805.

Hobbs' Pattern Padlock.

GALVANIZED.

2-Key'd.

	1½	1¾	2	2¼	2½	3 inch.
2-Lever	21/-	21/-	22/-	25/-	28/-	34/- per doz.

4 Lever 6/6 per doz. extra.

Above: The workforce at Lowe & Fletcher in around 1920. The firm made a wide range of locks, but specialised in ships locks, which needed to be especially corrosion resistant to withstand salt water. They would generally be made of brass or galvanised iron.

Left: A padlock from a Lowe & Fletcher catalogue of around 1900.

Opposite above: In the inter-war period Josiah Parkes Ltd emerged as one of the country's leading lock manufacturers. Having employed about 100 people before the First World War, by 1934 they were employing over 500. Success brought with it the rebuilding of much of the factory in Union Street, and in 1933 the erection of a stylish main office and warehouse in nearby Gower Street.

THE MAIN OFFICE AND WAREHOUSE

Below: A bird's eye view of Josiah Parkes' Union Works in Union Street. The small-scale domestic origins of the lock trade are very evident in this view. Josiah Parkes and his brother William were living here in 1861, Josiah at no.77 and William at no.78, with their warehouse in between. They were described as iron merchants and lock manufacturers at this date. Trinity Methodist Church, perhaps the largest of the town's nonconformist chapels, can be seen on the left of the view.

Japanning locks at Josiah Parkes in 1925. The women are coating locks with a protective layer of black lacquer or japan, to help prevent corrosion of the metal.

The fitting shop at Josiah Parkes in 1925. The various lock parts, which have previously been cast or pressed, are being assembled after filing and checking. Examples of the locksmith's typical small anvil or 'hubbin' can be seen set into the workbench tops.

The bobbing and polishing shop at Josiah Parkes in the 1920s. Banks of belt-driven wheels covered with felt would be used to polish parts such as lock cases. Spare bobbing wheels can be seen in racks at the back of the workshop.

The cabinet lock shop at Josiah Parkes in the mid-1920s. The locks are being checked and assembled and any imperfections from casting, which might impair the smooth action of the lock, removed by filing.

Cylinder lock assembly at Josiah Parkes in 1926. The rotating cylinder lock, or more correctly the pin tumbler lock, was developed by Linus Yale Jr in the United States in the 1860s, although the principle of the lock had been known to the ancient Egyptians. The cylinder lock was well suited to mass

production. Because the combination of tumblers was capable of almost infinite variation, the lock also offered excellent security. Josiah Parkes began making such locks in 1911.

Casting at Parkes' Portobello Foundry. The red-hot crucible is being raised by chains to enable the molten metal to be poured into one end of the casting box or 'flask'. Once cooled, the casting would be cleaned of any remaining sand. A range of metals was used in lockmaking including brass, malleable cast iron, gunmetal and manganese bronze. The choice of metal would depend largely on the purpose for which the lock was intended.

Walsall was of relatively minor importance in lock-making history when compared with Willenhall, but it did possess one very remarkable lock company. Walsall Locks & Cart Gear was established as a workers' co-operative in 1873, following the refusal of a local employer to reinstate three workers. It was a success from the beginning and an impressive factory was built in Neale Street in Birchills in 1892. In this view of around 1900, women are operating belt-driven presses in the foreground, with hand-operated fly presses at the rear. (Collection of Walsall Museums)

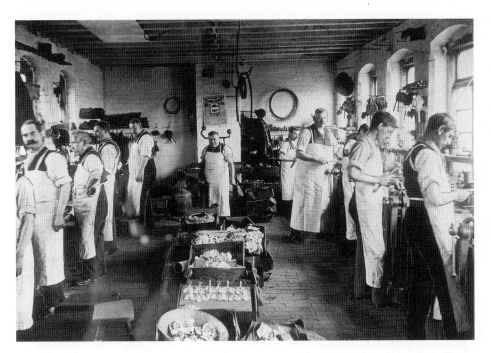

Locksmiths producing brass cabinet locks at Walsall Locks & Cart Gear, *c.*1900. The company had become the longest-established workers' co-operative in Britain when it went into receivership in 1985. (Collection of Walsall Museums)

An early Fordson tractor being used to drive the bobbing shop at Josiah Parkes during the Great Strike in 1926.

Willenhall's lock factories played an important part in munitions production during the Second World War, as they had in the First World War. These women are assembling fuses in 1945. As a special concession to married women, Josiah Parkes announced in 1943 that they might finish work half an hour early on three nights per week, 'for shopping'. Normal hours for women workers in the company were from 8.00a.m. to 6.00p.m., with an earlier finish on Saturdays.

Rebuilding part of the Yale factory in Wood Street in 1970. Locks have been made on this site for well over a century, and in 1872 Henry Vaughan was making rim and dead locks here. At the time of the redevelopment the site had nineteen different floor levels! The factory looks out across the Wood Street cemetery, where many of the leading figures of the lock industry are buried.

six

Town of
100 Trades

'... its chief strength and distinction is in the multitude, as well as in the variety, of its business enterprise.'
(Howard Clark, *Walsall Past and Present*, 1905)

Walsall has had an astonishing variety of trades for a town of its size. An official guide to *Walsall and its Industrial Advantages* published in 1936 listed a total of 183 trades, but even then admitted that the list was only '*fairly* comprehensive'.

Many of the town's specialist trades, such as the making of curry combs in Willenhall, nuts and bolts in Darlaston, or horse brasses and handbags in Walsall, can be grouped under the general headings of metalworking and leatherworking, and have already been discussed in previous chapters. These trades have, quite understandably, tended to dominate accounts of Walsall's industrial history, but alongside these two main groupings have existed an intriguing range of other trades not usually seen as being associated with Walsall or the Black Country. Among these 'hundred trades' are the manufacture of false teeth, spectacles, glue, polish, church organs, tents and camouflage nets, polo sticks, clogs, mineral water, wooden barrels and wheelbarrows, cardboard boxes, pickles, corsets and trusses, umbrellas, postage stamps, railway sleepers, canal boats, camera lenses, plastic jewellery, waterproof rugs, shaving brushes, embossed seals, and sausages. While some of these trades proved to be short-lived experiments, employing a handful of people at most, others such as brush making have proved to be of much longer duration, with a continuous history of over 200 years. Equally, while some of these trades have been of very local significance, others are or have been giants, serving international markets. Firms such as J.A. Crabtree, The Streetly Manufacturing Co., Walsall Lithographic and John Shannon & Sons have provided employment for thousands of men and women, and achieved national and international reputations in their respective fields.

Collectively Walsall's non-leather and non-metal trades have been vital to the local economy, giving it a remarkable degree of flexibility and resilience. It has been Walsall's great good fortune that it has never been a one-industry town, and that even as one trade has dwindled – as raw materials were exhausted, fashions or technology changed or markets were lost to foreign competitors – another has been rising in its place. The breadth of skills in the Borough has meant that local people have been well placed to respond to new opportunities, and diversity has been a source of real strength.

Opposite above: J.A. Crabtree opened his first factory, in Upper Rushall Street, in 1919, making electrical goods such as switches, plugs and sockets. The building had formerly been part of the saddlery works of John Leckie and Co. (All Crabtree photographs courtesy Allan Preston and the Crabtree Society)

Opposite below: Typical Crabtree switches from a 1925 catalogue.

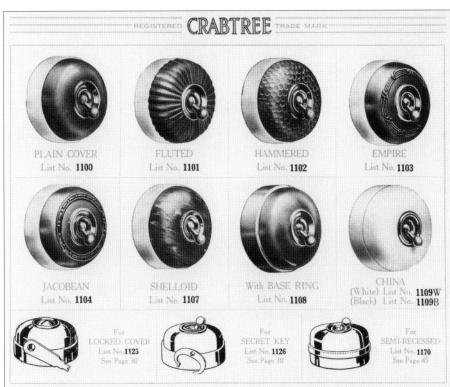

Within four years Crabtree was able to purchase an extensive greenfield site in Chuckery, about a mile from the town centre, where a state-of-the-art factory, the Lincoln Works, was built. The market for electrical goods was booming as more and more houses, offices and factories were connected to the mains; by 1938 two-thirds of all British homes were wired for electricity.

John Ashworth Crabtree in his oak-panelled office at the Lincoln Works. He was a man of exceptional vision and energy, making the company the leader in its field, and Crabtree a household name. Returning from a business trip to the United States he caught pneumonia and died in 1935 at the age of only forty-nine.

Women assembling switch gear at Crabtree in about 1930. For much of the twentieth century the company was one of the largest private sector employers in the town, with a local workforce of over 2,000 people (and around 3,800 worldwide). The firm had a reputation for being a good employer.

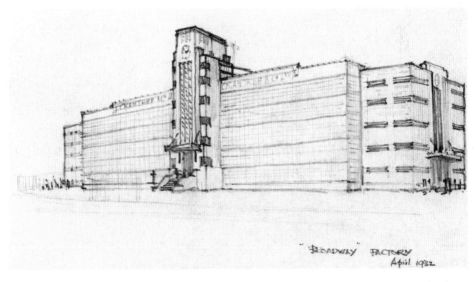

A previously unpublished sketch in J.A. Crabtree's own hand, dated 1932, which suggests that he had ambitious plans to extend the Lincoln Works and create a splendid new Art Deco frontage facing onto the ring road, which had been renamed the Broadway the previous year.

Left: Operating a moulding machine at Crabtree in 1933. The factory was largely self-contained and most components were manufactured on site. A patented heat-resistant plastic, which had been developed by Crabtree's technicians, named 'Jacelite', was used in the manufacture of many of the company's products.

Below: A group of Crabtree employees celebrate the visit of The Queen to the Lincoln Works in 1962. The firm was flourishing thanks to the post-war housing and consumer goods boom that ensured a healthy demand for its products.

Right: Walsall is not a noted centre of the clothing trade, yet surprisingly at one time over 3,000 people were employed in the Borough in making garments of various kinds. This advertisement, dating from 1916, suggests that at least one local company was engaged in producing overalls for women workers employed in wartime munitions work.

Below: Walsall's largest clothing manufacturer was John Shannon & Sons. At its peak in around 1900 the firm employed over 2,000 people at its George Street factory. Like so many of Walsall's notable companies it was founded by an 'incomer', in this instance a Scotsman. The Royal Commission on Labour noted in 1893 that the expansion of the town's clothing trade had made the 'girls' more choosy as they no longer had to rely upon the saddlery and bridle trade for work! (Photograph courtesy T. Gameson & Sons)

The Holtshill Manufacturing Co., Ltd.

St. Paul's, WALSALL

Manufacturers of
OVERALLS, APRONS, PINAFORES & SKIRTS
Also MEN'S SHIRTS

CABLE YOUR WANTS

OVERALL No. A 200

Prices for Overalls, as sketches,
11/- to **35/-** per dozen

CONTRACTORS TO H.M. GOVERNMENT

EXPORTERS TO
ALL PARTS OF THE WORLD

OVERALL No. A 169

Above: In 1922 there were six clothing manufacturers in the town, some of them probably founded by former Shannon employees. Norton & Proffitt, seen here in about 1920, was located in Midland Road. (Photograph courtesy Mrs Evans)

Right: Brush making has a tradition of over 200 years in Walsall, and brushes are still made in the town today. These dog brushes are from a catalogue of Messrs Bradnack & Son of 1936.

Opposite above: Making badger-hair shaving brushes, thought to be at Messrs Bradnack & Son's factory in Birmingham Road in the 1960s. The women are trimming the hair with scissors before securing it in the stocks of the brushes, which appear to be of ivory. (Photograph courtesy Margaret Foster, copyright *Walsall Observer*)

Opposite below: Another view inside the same factory, which was sited next door to the Wheatsheaf pub. This craftsman is shaping the stocks for shaving brushes, using a lathe and chisels. Messrs Bradnack & Son was eventually taken over by Vale Bros, who continue to manufacture brushes in Walsall, and are Royal Warrant Holders, supplying horse-grooming brushes to the Royal Household. (Photograph courtesy Margaret Foster, copyright *Walsall Observer*)

Telephone No. 6039.   ESTABLISHED 1837.   Works:
Telegraphic Address—   TANTARRA STREET and
"ROPE," WALSALL.   ——   SELBORNE STREET.

J. HAWLEY & Co.,

GOODALL STREET, WALSALL,

MANUFACTURERS OF

ROPES, TWINES, CORDS,

SACKS, HALTERS, PLOUGH REINS, &c.

CART,   HORSE

WAGGON,   CLOTHS,

and   SACKING,

RICK   CANVAS,

SHEETS.   &c.

TENTS AND MARQUEES

FOR SALE OR HIRE.

CONTRACTORS TO HER MAJESTY'S GOVERNMENT.

PRICE LISTS ON APPLICATION.   PRICE LISTS ON APPLICATION.

We claim to have the largest Stock of Tents in the Midland Counties.
The *Midland Evening News* stated that our Tents at the Wolverhampton
Flower Show were the largest canvas erections ever seen.

JOHN HAWLEY & Co., Goodall St., Walsall.

Left: John Hawley started out in 1837 as a rope maker. The company later opened ropewalks in Tantarra Street and Selborne Street, the latter remembered by the footpath still known to Chuckery residents as 'The Ropewalk'. The firm eventually moved to Bloxwich Road, and latterly specialised in making tents.

Below: John Hawley's son, John James, set up in business in Park Street in 1860, making rope and canvas products in rivalry to his father's company. A new factory incorporating a ropewalk was built in Lichfield Road in 1909, of which the entrance is seen here, with some fine terracotta detailing. Amongst the firm's products were tarpaulins, feeding nets, horse and cattle clothing, garden furniture and 'Lichfield' brand tents; by the 1980s they were probably Britain's largest tent manufacturer.

Right: Penkridge Ceramics was founded in 1984, and has been based in Walsall since 1993, making a range of fruit and vegetable 'portraits' in semi-porcelain clay. Their work is renowned for its remarkably lifelike appearance, the result of constant experimentation with glazes and matting agents, and meticulous attention to the finish of each piece. This image shows some of their striking unglazed pieces.

Below: Walsall's near neighbour, Bilston, is a celebrated centre of the British enamel industry. These examples, made for Halcyon Days, were cast from original models produced by the Walsall sculptor, Richard Roberts. Richard has produced over 300 original designs for this company since 1988. Halcyon Days is one of only seven UK companies to currently hold all four Royal Warrants.

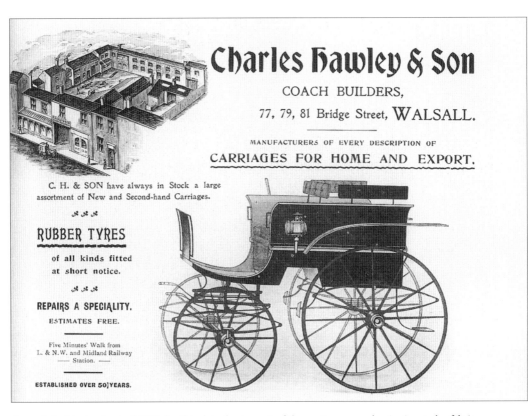

A coach builder's advert of 1905; by this date the impact of the motorcar was beginning to be felt in many of Walsall's trades. Charles Hawley & Sons soon merged with a rival company, and by the First World War the firm was listed as 'Hawley Mills and Co., Carriage and Motor Car Body Manufacturers'.

Walsall has an extensive network of canals, and boat building is a long-established trade which survives to this day. Ernie Thomas operated a boat-building yard at Birchills Warf, seen here in an advertisement from around 1956. He was a successful entrepreneur who seized the opportunity created by the opening of coal-fired power stations in the Midlands to build up a fleet of 300 canal boats, carrying coal for the CEGB.

The world's first self-adhesive postage stamp was developed, designed and printed by Walsall Security Printers for the government of Sierra Leone in 1964. Established in 1894 as the Walsall Lithographic Co., the company is today one of the world's largest producers of stamps and security documents, and its Wednesbury Road factory is a familiar local landmark.

The Highgate Brewery in Sandymount Road began brewing in 1899, and is Walsall's last surviving brewery. In 1925 there were seven breweries in the town. Highgate was taken over by Mitchells & Butlers in 1939, at which time it was operating over fifty licensed premises. Its survival seems to have been largely thanks to the local popularity of the dark mild ale produced here.

George and Marie Pelari came to England from Italy in 1895, setting up in business in Stafford Street making ice cream. George can be seen on the left of this view taken at the back of the factory in Bate Street around 1905, with Marie in the middle, holding her young daughter Polly. George was a talented

...arpenter and made all of the ice-cream carts himself. The entry leads to the workshop of T. Finegan, saddler
— close to the site of the present-day Leather Museum. (Photograph courtesy Mr Sanders)

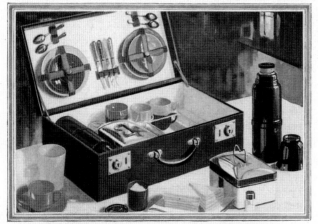

BEATL–for Brighter Picnics

For comfort and convenience in picnicking, insist on Beatl. No more breakages. No soggy paper plates and cups to bury. The bright Beatl fittings go home to come again another day. All you have to do is to throw them into your car and pack up at your leisure.

Beatl is light in weight, but immensely durable. The cups nest compactly into each other—so do the tumblers—the very thing for motoring, river or garden.

The Beatl Luncheon and Tea Case illustrated above (No. 2668/4B) provides for four persons. It includes 2 Thermos of the latest type with canisters made entirely of Beatl. PRICE: £7 11s. 0d. (or, with No. 16 Thermos £7 7s. 0d.).

2734/2—Tea Case for two ;	49/6
2734/4—Tea Case for four ;	69/6
2715/4—Tea and Luncheon Case for four ;	115/6
S.1—Leather Case with shoulder strap, containing Thermos, 2 tumblers and sandwich tin ;	39/6
F.H.1—Ditto, no sandwich tin ;	21/-
F.C.1—Ditto, in canvas case ;	16/6

Many other selections for lunch or tea in Bandalasta, M.L. or Linga Longa Wares are obtainable at the Beatl Shop, 219, Regent Street, London (Tel. Mayfair 4352) and at leading Stores throughout the country.

British Industrial Plastics of Oldbury discovered the world's first white commercial moulding powder for plastics in 1926. The new material, which was named Beetle, represented a breakthrough in plastics as it could be produced in a range of colours. It was also odourless and tasteless and therefore ideally suited for use with food and cosmetics. Three years later the firm acquired The Streetly Manufacturing Co., and began producing its own plastic mouldings, such as mugs and picnic sets. 'Beetleware' or 'Beatl' proved to be a great hit, with Woolworths rapidly becoming a major customer.

The company's factory at Aldridge Road, Streetly, was situated in the midst of open country, part of the original Coldfield, as this view of 1936 demonstrates. Walsall Corporation laid on a special bus service for the workforce, few of whom would have owned cars at this date. (Photograph courtesy Mike Butler/BIP)

Above: A row of presses in one of the moulding shops at Streetly in 1949. The moulder nearest the camera is making Beetle plates. Unable to find the quality of presses they required, in 1949 BIP set up a subsidiary company, BIPEL, to manufacture hydraulic presses specifically for plastic moulding. BIP was probably unique in the history of the British plastics industry in that it made not only the raw material, but also a range of finished goods to its own designs, as well as the presses in which they were moulded. (Photograph courtesy Mike Butler/BIP)

Below: The huge success of Beetle was followed in the 1950s and '60s by further success with melamine products. BIP launched a subsidiary named Gaydon in 1961 to market its own range of melamine tableware. Although never cheap, Gaydon products had an excellent reputation, being light, colourful, and resistant to chipping and cracking. The designs, by A.H. 'Woody' Woodfull, were simple and sculptural and perfectly caught the spirit of the age. (Photograph courtesy Mike Butler/BIP)

Other titles published by Tempus

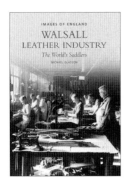

Walsall Leather Industry The World's Saddlers
MICHAEL GLASSON

For nearly two hundred years, Walsall has been a major centre of the leather industry, exporting a variety of horse equipment to several countries. Its seventy or so saddlery firms have an international reputation for their products, and not surprisingly the town has sometimes been called the saddlery 'capital' of the world.

07524 2793 8

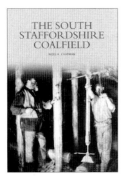

The South Staffordshire Coalfield
NIGEL CHAPMAN

At one time, South Staffordshire had the finest bed of coal that had ever been discovered. This book relates the history of the long-gone Black Country collieries that flourished in the age of the Industrial Revolution, and which did a lot to create the West Midlands that exists today.

07524 3102 1

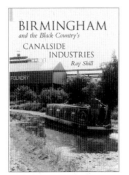

Birmingham and the Black Country's Canalside Industries
RAY SHILL

Coal mining and iron working prospered in the West Midlands in the nineteenth century, after the development of local industry, in particular metalworking and the use of coal, iron and limestone. This illustrated volume examines the canalside industries of Birmingham and the Black Country, looking at iron, coal, gas, electricity, bricks and firebricks, and railway interchange, plus some of the more modern trades.

07524 3262 1

A Guide to the Buildings of Walsall
PETER ARNOLD

This book describes and illustrates some of the most historically important architecture to be seen in Walsall today and will serve as a useful guide for those wishing to explore and learn more about the borough's history through its buildings.

07524 2498 X

If you are interested in purchasing other books published by Tempus, or in case you have difficulty finding any Tempus books in your local bookshop, you can also place orders directly through our website

www.tempus-publishing.com